RELISH
SCOTLAND

Original recipes from the region's finest chefs

First Published 2010
By Relish Publications
Shield Green Farm, Tritlington,
Northumberland NE61 3DX

ISBN 978-0-9564205-2-7

Publisher: Duncan L Peters
General Manager: Teresa Baughan
Marketing and PR: Ria Parkin
Design: room501 publishing
Photography: NR Photography & KG Photography
Printed By: Balto Print Ltd, Stratford,
London E15 2TF

RELISH
PUBLICATIONS.CO.UK

004
CONTENTS

DESSERTS

DESSERTS	RESTAURANTS	
Chocolate and Raspberry Napoleon	Bistro du Vin	012-021
Polenta Cake, Cherry Compote and Honey & Lavender Ice Cream	Blackaddie Country House Hotel	022-031
Cannelloni of Chocolate and Cardamom	Castle Terrace Restaurant	032-041
Tiramisu	Cucina	042-051
Kesree Bhath	The Dakhin	052-061
Chawal Ki Kheer	The Dhabba	062-071
White Chocolate and Raspberry Dessert, Mousse, Bonbon, and Soup	Dalhousie Castle	072-081
Poached Mountain Peach, Lemon Thyme Curd, Raspberry Ripple Parfait	The Dining Room	082-091
Strawberry Dish	The Forth Floor Restaurant at Harvey Nichols	092-101
Milk Chocolate and Grand Marnier Mousse with Orange Curd Ice Cream	Glenapp Castle	102-111
Apple Tart Tatin	The Grill Room at the Square	112-121
Morello Cherries with Vanilla Sponge, Pistachio, Kirsch Foam and Cherry Sorbet	The Horseshoe Inn	122-131
Ecclefechan Tart	Martin Wishart at Loch Lomond	132-141
Coffee Caramel Mousse, Caramel Espuma, Vanilla Butter Ice Cream	Michael Caine's at ABode Glasgow	142-151
Gateau	The Plumed Horse	152-161

006 CONTENTS

DESSERTS

RESTAURANTS

INTRODUCTION
WITH
NICK NAIRN

Scotland's best-known chef, Nick is in high demand as chef, consultant and personality and is a prominent spokesperson on diet, healthy eating and Scottish produce. He has published ten cookery books and appeared on countless TV shows, including Great British Menu, Ready Steady Cook and Saturday Kitchen. He also regularly presents foodie sections on Landward and The One Show. Nick owns and teaches at his acclaimed Nick Nairn Cook School on the stunning shores of the Lake of Menteith in The Trossachs. His Nick Nairn Consultancy, too, goes from strength to strength, with a supermarket food range and partnerships with Hilton at Dunblane Hydro, the charity Erskine and many more. Nick has also taken to blogging. Catch up with him at www.nicknairn.tv/blog.

I feel very proud to be championing this book. Scotland is incredibly fortunate to have the best produce on the planet, and that's no exaggeration. The sheer variety and quality of ingredients available to chefs here is phenomenal. We've got beautiful, unpolluted oceans, brimming with lobster, scallops, langoustine, crab, mussels, oysters and all manner of fish. Our fields abound with happy native-breed cattle such as Highland, Belted Galloway, Aberdeen Angus – not to mention some stunning dairy herds and hill lamb. We've got gourmet game all over the shop, from pheasant and grouse to roe deer. And to top all that we're the world's biggest producer of succulent berries and soft fruit. Then there's the mushrooms, asparagus, tatties, and more. It's an amazing natural larder.

And what's really fantastic is that in the last 20 years, we've upped our cooking game too. The chefs and restaurants featured in these pages use these natural ingredients with an instinctive understanding of how to make the best of what's in season. Because that's what great Scottish cooking is about – making the produce the star. People like Geoffrey Smeddle at the Peat Inn, Tom Lewis at Monachyle Mhor, Tony Borthwick at The Plumed Horse, Tom Kitchin at The Kitchin in Edinburgh, Claire Macdonald at Kinloch Lodge up on Skye – all the people in this book – are doing just that and producing food to sublime standards.

It's not only chefs who make Scotland an awesome food destination, either, it's our local producers. The farmers, fishermen, dairy workers and butchers, people like the expert salmon smokers up at Loch Duart, my fab local butcher Jonathan Honeyman at The Aberfoyle Butcher, or Graham's Dairies also here in the Trossachs. You'll find producers like these all over Scotland, helping us all to eat well.

Our stunning surroundings play a part, too. Being near the places where the food comes from, our lochs, coasts, hills and rivers, also influences our eating experience. For me, the best time to think about food and cooking is when I'm out in the countryside, walking in the hills or mountain biking. And I think this is what all of us cooking in Scotland have a feel for, the connection between our food and the land it's come from. It not only shapes and defines who we are, but what we eat and the way we cook.

Happy eating.
Nick Nairn

010
RESTAURANTS IN THE BORDERS, EDINBURGH AND GLASGOW

WHERE TO LOCATE THEM

1. BISTRO DU VIN, Hotel du Vin, 11 Bristo Place, Edinburgh EH1 1EZ

2. BLACKADDIE COUNTRY HOUSE HOTEL, Blackaddie Road, Sanquhar, Dumfries DG4 6JJ

3. CASTLE TERRACE, 33–35 Castle Terrace, Edinburgh EH1 2EL

4. CUCINA, 1 George IV Bridge, Edinburgh EH1 1AD

5. THE DAKHIN, First Floor, 89 Candleriggs, Merchant City, Glasgow G1 1NP

6. THE DHABBA, 44 Candleriggs, Merchant City, Glasgow G1 1LE

7. DALHOUSIE CASTLE, Bonnyrigg, Edinburgh EH19 3JB

8. THE DINING ROOM, 28 Queen Street, Edinburgh EH2 1JX

9. THE FORTH FLOOR at HARVEY NICOLS, 30–34 St Andrew Square, Edinburgh E2 2AD

10. GLENAPP CASTLE, Ballantrae, Ayrshire KA26 0NZ

11. THE GRILL ROOM at THE SQUARE, 29 Royal Exchange Square, Glasgow G1 3AJ

12. THE HORSESHOE INN, Eddleston, Peebles EH45 8QP

13. MARTIN WISHART at LOCH LOMOND, Cameron House, Dumbartonshire G83 3QZ

14. MICHAEL CAINES at ABODE GLASGOW, 129 Bath Street, Glasgow G2 2SX

15. THE PLUMED HORSE, 50–54 Henderson Street, Edinburgh EH6 6DE

16. ROGANO, 11 Exchange Place, Glasgow G1 3AN

17. WEDGWOOD THE RESTAURANT, The Royal Mile, 267 Canongate, Edinburgh EH8 8BQ

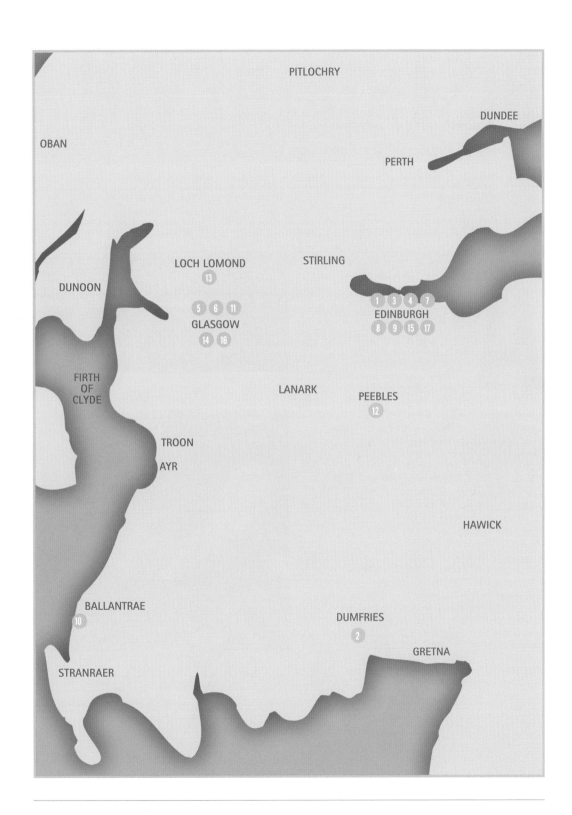

PITLOCHRY

DUNDEE

OBAN

PERTH

LOCH LOMOND
13

STIRLING

DUNOON

5 6 11
GLASGOW
14 16

1 3 4 7
EDINBURGH
8 9 15 17

FIRTH
OF
CLYDE

LANARK

PEEBLES
12

TROON

AYR

HAWICK

BALLANTRAE
10

DUMFRIES
2

GRETNA

STRANRAER

012
BISTRO DU VIN

Hotel du Vin, 11 Bristo Place, Edinburgh EH1 1EZ

0131 247 4900
www.hotelduvin.com

Another new addition to the Hotel du Vin family of luxury boutique hotels, Hotel du Vin Edinburgh is nestled deep in Edinburgh's Old Town and only a short walk from the historic Royal Mile. Neighbouring the famous Bedlam theatre, the Hotel occupies the site of a former asylum while its 47 timelessly furnished rooms and stunning suites provide the perfect base to explore Edinburgh's historic and cultural heritage.

A relaxing haven, this hotel offers the trademark Bistro du Vin with mezzanine bar serving the finest classic European cuisine. This is home to our award winning Chef, Matt Powell. Having been with the hotel since its opening in December 2008, Matt has already made a big impact winning Hotel du Vin and Malmaison Chef of the Year 2009. Matt trained in London at the Savoy, being taught by the great Anton Edelmann. He is influenced and inspired to produce great British food with a French twist, his signature dish being Isle of Mull soufflé.

Hotel du Vin also offers alfresco and private dining with bespoke menus created upon request, an outdoor heated cigar shack, whisky snug and intriguing Laroche tasting room where you can be taken on a pilgrimage around the world's finest vineyards by the Head Sommelier without having to leave the room. The hotel also holds regular wine dinners bringing Matt's innovative cuisine together with a selection of wines presented by experts from some of the most exceptional wineries around the world.

For more information go to www.hotelduvin.com.

A relaxing haven, this hotel offers the trademark Bistro du Vin with mezzanine bar serving the finest classic European cuisine

SNAILS WITH BONE MARROW, PARSLEY AND BLACK PEPPER

SERVES 4

Ingredients

48 snail shells
large glass of white wine
large pinch chopped herbs
salt and pepper

Snail Butter

450g bone marrow (softened)
50g peeled garlic (finely chopped)
75g flat leaf parsley (leaves only)
25g breadcrumbs
50g cracked black pepper
1½ tsp salt
¼ tsp cayenne
5 drops of Tabasco sauce
1 baguette

Method

For the bone marrow (which you should be able to get from any good butcher if you pre order). Beat together with the garlic in a mixer. Blanch half the parsley in boiling water for a few seconds then drain and refresh. Chop with the remaining parsley as fine as possible. Add the remaining ingredients and beat together until thoroughly blended. Chill.

Drain the snails and put in a pan with the wine herbs and seasoning. Bring up to a simmer and cook for 10 minutes or so. Leave to cool in the liquor then drain.

Using your thumb push a small amount (half tsp) of the bone marrow mix into the bottom of the snail shell then insert the snail with its curved and pointed end uppermost. Gently push it further down into the shell and then top up with more bone marrow mix (three times as much as before). Smooth off.

Place in the serving dishes as horizontal as possible, put on a baking tray and cook on the top shelf of the oven for 15-20 minutes until bubbling.

To serve

Serve with crusty baguette.

DANDELION AND BURDOCH BAKED HAM HOCK, CURLY KALE AND SWEETCORN PUDDING

SERVES 4

Ingredients

4 ea hamhock
2 ltr dandelion and burdoch
1 ea onion
2 ea carrots
1 head celery
1 head curly kale
10g treacle
10g mustard powder
10g brown sugar

Sweetcorn Pudding

5 ea eggs
800g sweetcorn kernals
250ml milk
250ml cream
150g plain flour
½ tsp salt

Parsley Sauce

250ml ham stock (take from the liquid
you cooked ham hocks in)
20g butter
20g flour
1 bunch flat leaf parsley

Method

Roughly chop all vegetables apart from the curly kale and place in the pan with the dandelion and burdoch, bring to the boil. When boiling place the ham hocks in the dandelion and burdoch pan and simmer for three hours or until the hock meat can easily come off the bone.

For the sweetcorn pudding

Butter and flour a round cake tin, mix all ingredients together until it is a thick sauce consistency, then add to the tin and bake for 1hr 15 minutes at 160°C. When cooked rest for 1hr and cut into 8 portions

For the parsley sauce

Make a roux with the butter and flour in a heavy based pan and cook out for 10 minutes on a low heat. Slowly add ham stock continuously stirring until you get a smooth sauce. Pick the leaves off the parsley stalks and with a food processor blitz through the sauce until your sauce is green. Pass through a sieve and set to one side.

When ham hocks are cooked take out of the dandelion and burdoch liquor and trim up all excess fat so you can see a bit of the bone and there is just a thin layer left on the meat.

To serve

Brush ham hock with treacle and then sprinkle with brown sugar and mustard powder. Bake in oven for 10 minutes at 190°C, 5 minutes in add the portioned sweetcorn pudding. While this is happening chop curly kale and blanche in boiling salted water for a couple of minutes, gently warm sauce up in a pan. When everything is cooked arrange on the plate.

CHOCOLATE AND RASPBERRY NAPOLEON
SERVES 4

Ingredients

2 punnets of raspberries

Feuillantine

100g milk chocolate
200g praline paste
125g sweet feuillantine wafer biscuit

Chocolate Cream

100ml double cream
100g dark chocolate
100g hazelnut spread

Method

For the feuillantine

Break up the chocolate and melt with the praline paste in a heatproof mixing bowl over simmering water. Crush up the wafers take the chocolate and praline mixture off the heat.

Line a rectangular tray with greaseproof paper and then spread mix into tray, make a thin rectangle, chill in freezer for 20 minutes.

For the chocolate cream

Break up the chocolate, bring double cream to the boil, remove to one side and add the chocolate and hazelnut, spread and stir until completely melted.

Cut feuillantine into 12x4cm rectangles, spread a layer of chocolate cream and then place a layer of raspberries, repeat this and then place one layer of feuillantine on top.

To serve

Serve with double cream.

022
BLACKADDIE COUNTRY HOUSE HOTEL

Blackaddie Road, Sanquhar, Dumfries DG4 6JJ

01659 50270
www.blackaddiehotel.co.uk

Food, service and great genuinely warm hospitality are at the very heart of what Blackaddie House is all about, the food is simply outstanding.

Owned by Ian and Jane McAndrew, Blackaddie has been setting enviable standards since they bought the hotel in 2007. Ian, formerly the youngest Englishman to be awarded a coveted Michelin Star presides over the kitchens where absolutely everything is made in house from the finest of ingredients, many of which are local.

Jane oversees the front of house and ensures that guests feel at home from the moment they arrive. Together they have made Blackaddie House Hotel a real destination in what is a beautiful yet little known area of Scotland.

Set in two acres of stunning gardens that have the most amazing floral displays imaginable throughout the summer. Sitting alongside and overlooking the river Nith, a fine salmon river, the hotel is a haven of peace and tranquillity in the outskirts of the Royal Burgh of Sanquhar.

The area is one of quiet natural beauty while being perfectly placed to access many places. Only 1 hour from Glasgow and 90 minutes from Edinburgh, 30 miles from Ayr and Kilmarnock with Dumfries 28 miles, even Carlisle is just over an hour away, there is much to see and do. Apart from the obvious fishing benefits being so close to the river there is also Drumlanrig Castle and Dumfries House close by. Sited on the edge of the Southern Upland Way, if you like walking with some fantastic unspoilt countryside in all directions. The 7 Stanes mountain bike trails for those that like cycling extreme are not far away and the beautiful Galloway Hills are literally round the corner. For those wanting more outdoor sports we can organise shooting and stalking in this game rich area.

Blackaddie offers a unique dining experience but apart from the fantastic food what sets Blackaddie apart is the relaxed friendly staff, great service but not too formal!

CAULIFLOWER PANNA COTTA WITH A SALAD OF GOATS' CHEESE, BEETROOT AND BALSAMIC RASPBERRIES

SERVES 4

Ingredients

185ml double cream
185ml milk
160g cauliflower
10g sliced shallots
1 clove garlic crushed
dash Worcestershire sauce
seasoning
3 leaves of gelatine
150g cooked beetroot
40g mixed baby salad leaves
16 fresh raspberries
40g crumbled goats cheese
olive oil
20ml reduced balsamic vinegar

Method

Chop the cauliflower and add to the milk and cream in a saucepan, add the shallots, garlic, Worcester sauce, season to taste and bring to the boil Simmer gently until the cauliflower is fully cooked.

Soak the leaves of gelatine in cold water till soft.

Transfer to a liquidiser and process until smooth; pass through a fine strainer or muslin. Stir in the gelatine and make sure it is completely dissolved.

Cling film the bases of 4 moulds and pour in the mix. Transfer to the refrigerator till set.

Cut the beetroot into batons.

To dress

Turn the cauliflower panna cotta moulds upside down on the plate, using a blow torch lightly warm each one so the panna cotta slips out. Lightly toss the leaves in the olive oil and season.

To serve

Arrange these and the beetroot batons and the crumbled goats cheese in front of the panna cotta.

Pipe a little balsamic vinegar into each raspberry and arrange these in the salad.

HALIBUT ON A KEDGEREE RISOTTO WITH SOFT BOILED QUAILS EGGS AND CONFIT CHICKEN

SERVES 4

Ingredients

4 x 130g halibut portions
100g chick peas
95g natural smoked haddock fillet
chicken leg boned and skinned
20g sea salt
100g duck fat
1 clove of garlic
10g chopped shallot
1 clove crushed garlic
50ml olive oil
100g Arborio rice
5g curry powder
sprig fresh thyme,
50ml dry white wine
400ml water mixed with 200ml milk
8 quails eggs
80g cold unsalted butter
55g grated parmesan
25g chopped parsley
20g micro leaves
40ml veal jus

Method

For the confit

Soak the chick peas in cold water overnight.

Sprinkle the chicken leg with the sea salt and leave for 12 hours. Wash off the salt, cover with the duck fat and add the clove of garlic, and cook as slowly as possible (at around 70°c) until the meat is tender (about 4 hours). Once cooked, remove the chicken from the fat, wrap in cling film then press between two trays till cold and set. Cut into a neat dice allowing 5 pieces per portion.

Cover the chick peas with water and simmer till cooked, drain.

For the risotto

Sweat the shallots and crushed garlic for a couple of minutes in 30ml of the oil. Add the rice, curry powder and thyme, sweat for a further 2 minutes. Add the white wine and reduce till almost gone. Add the smoked haddock and gradually add water/milk mix stirring often and simmer until just cooked and almost all of the liquid has been absorbed.

For the quails eggs

Plunge the quails eggs in rapidly boiling water for 2½ minutes then remove immediately into iced water. Gently peel the eggs.

Heat the remaining oil in a frying pan, when hot add 40g of the cold butter, when sizzling season the fish and pan fry both sides till lightly browned and cooked, remove and keep warm.

Finish the risotto by stirring in the remaining butter, the parmesan, the parsley and chickpeas, continue to stir until all the butter and parmesan has melted.

To serve

Spoon the risotto onto the plates and place a piece of fish on top. Arrange the micro cress in 5 piles around the plate and top each one with a piece of chicken. Drop the quails eggs into hot water for a few seconds to reheat then place two on each plate. Drizzle with the jus.

POLENTA CAKE, CHERRY COMPOTE AND HONEY & LAVENDER ICE CREAM

SERVES 8

Ingredients

200g butter
200g golden caster sugar
200g ground almonds
100g polenta
3 eggs
4 lemons
1 tsp baking powder
90g extra tablespoons golden caster sugar

Ice Cream

300ml milk
300ml double cream
90g caster sugar
6 egg yolks
60g honey
good pinch dried lavender

Cherry Compote

300g stoned fresh cherries
75ml sugar syrup
25ml vodka

Mascarpone Cream

75g mascarpone cheese
50ml whipped cream
½ lemon

Method

For the polenta

In a bowl beat the butter and sugar until light and fluffy.

Add in the eggs one by one - beat well. Add in the remaining ground almonds and beat well, stir in the polenta and baking powder.

Grate in the zest of one of the lemons and the juice of half a lemon.

Mix well and then scrape the mixture into an 8 inch oblong cake tin.

Bake in an oven preheated to 170°C for between 45 minutes to an hour.

Grate the rind of two lemons and extract the juice from the remaining lemons.

Place the rind and the juice in a small saucepan with the 6 tablespoons of sugar. Stir well then heat until dissolved.

When the cake is cooked, remove it from the oven and prick all over with a skewer - immediately pour the lemon syrup over the cake and let it soak it. It will seem like there is a lot, but it will all soak in!

For the ice cream

Combine the milk, cream and half the sugar for the ice cream in a pan with the lavender and honey, gently bring to the boil. Whisk the egg yolks and remaining sugar until thick, pour the boiled milk mixture onto the egg yolks whisking well, strain into a clean pan and gently heat till it thickens, remove and chill. When cold, churn in an ice cream machine.

For the compote

Place the stoned cherries in a saucepan with the sugar syrup and vodka, bring to the boil and simmer for a minute or two until the cherries are cooked. Drain the cherries then reduce the liquid until thickened, return the cherries to it.

Zest and juice the ½ lemon, mix the zest and juice into the mascarpone with the whipped cream.

To serve

Heat the slices of polenta cake in the microwave for a few seconds, spoon the cherries around, top with the mascarpone cream and place a scoop of ice cream on the cake.

032
CASTLE TERRACE RESTAURANT

33-35 Castle Terrace, Edinburgh EH1 2EL

0131 229 1222
www.castleterracerestaurant.com

The Kitchin

Castle Terrace Restaurant

Since opening its doors in June 2006, Michaela and Tom Kitchin's eponymous restaurant The Kitchin, in Leith, Edinburgh has taken the food and restaurant industry by storm. The restaurant was awarded a prestigious Michelin star shortly after opening and was followed by a collection of additional awards.

In July 2010, the team behind The Kitchin and Chef Proprietor Dominic Jack opened a new city centre sister restaurant called Castle Terrace offering Scottish French cuisine, based on a menu reflecting Dominic Jack's many years of training in some of the world's best kitchens.

Scottish-born chefs Tom Kitchin and Dominic Jack began their careers together at the prestigious Gleneagles Hotel and followed similar career paths working alongside some of the world's 3-Michelin star master chefs for over 13 years – Tom with legendary Pierre Koffmann and Alain Ducasse and Dominic with Michel Perraud and Alain Solivérès.

With their shared philosophy 'From Nature to Plate' both restaurants present menus that are always seasonal and rely on the best suppliers in Scotland to provide the highest quality, freshest, flavoursome produce there is. The passionate chefs pride themselves on the fact that all of the produce arrive at the restaurants daily straight off the land or shores of Scotland.

Both The Kitchin and Castle Terrace offer a modern, relaxed and welcoming atmosphere.

While guests at The Kitchin can watch the chefs at work through the kitchen window while dining, Castle Terrace boasts a unique chance for guests to observe the kitchen in action while enjoying a glass of champagne or aperitif before dining.

In July 2010, The Kitchin launched its new city centre sister restaurant Castle Terrace, with chef proprietor Dominic Jack at the helm. Castle Terrace follows the same shared philosophy 'From Nature to Plate', presenting menus that are always seasonal and relying on the best suppliers in Scotland to provide the highest quality, freshest, flavoursome produce there is around

HOME-MADE POTATO GNOCCHI, SERVED WITH A FREE RANGE POACHED EGG AND WATERCRESS SOUP

SERVES 4

Ingredients

Watercress Soup

500g watercress
½ onion
150ml chicken stock
50g butter
50g cream

Poached Egg

4 eggs
distilled vinegar

Gnocchi (Serves 10)

500g potato
1 egg
1 egg yolk
100g flour
salt
pepper
10 basil leaves

To Dress

micro watercress
pink peppercorns
salt

Method

For the soup

Sweat onion in butter for 10 minutes without colouration.

Pick watercress leaves and blanch for 1 minute in boiling water and then refresh.

Take the watercress from ice and squeeze out water then add to onions.

Add chicken stock and bring to boil.

Blend thoroughly in blender.

Season to taste.

Whip the cream and add at the last minute.

For the poached egg

Place water in a large pan and bring to simmer and add vinegar.

Break eggs into water and leave for approx 3 minutes until cooked.

For the gnocchi

Bake potatoes in oven for 1½ hours at 180°C.

Cut in half, remove potato from skin and pass through sieve.

Mix with egg and basil and add the flour.

Cut into small balls and then neatly shape using the back of a fork.

Poach in boiling salted water until gnocchi rises to surface.

Remove on to tray and leave to cool.

Pan fry in olive oil until golden.

To serve

Place gnocchi in the middle of a plate.

Put the egg on top and sprinkle with salt, pepper and watercress.

Serve soup on the side.

ROASTED FILLET OF WILD NORTH SEA LING, SERVED WITH A SQUID RISOTTO AND LETTUCE PURÉE

SERVES 4

Ingredients

4 x 150g ling

Lettuce Purée

½ onion
5 mini gem lettuce
50ml fish stock
10g whipped cream

Risotto

30g shallots
100g spelt grain
50ml white wine
1lt fish stock
10g squid ink
50g parmesan cheese
20ml whipped cream
The heart of 1 mini gem lettuce – thinly cut

Squid Tempura

2 small squid cut into rings
70g cornflour
40g vodka

Method

For the fish

Place fish in non stick pan, skin side down, on high heat until skin starts to crisp.

Place pan in oven at 180°C until fish is cooked.

For the purée

Sweat onion and butter for 10 minutes without colouration.

Pick lettuce and blanche for 1 minute in boiling water and then refresh.

Take the lettuce from ice and squeeze out water.

Add to onions.

Add chicken stock and bring to boil.

Blend thoroughly in blender.

Season to taste.

Whip the cream and add at the last minute.

For the risotto

Sweat shallots in olive oil.

Add spelt and deglaze with white wine until dry.

Add 200ml of fish stock and cook until dry.

Add fish stock as needed.

Cook for 45 minutes or until al dente.

Finish risotto with parmesan, butter, whipped cream, squid ink and lettuce.

For the tempura

Mix vodka and cornflour and add water until there is a thick consistency.

Add salt and crushed black pepper.

Add squid and then deep fry at 180°C until crispy.

To dress

Make a ring of lettuce sauce on a plate.

Place the risotto in the middle and place fish on top.

Put the crispy squid around and add a few leaves of roquette salad.

CANNELLONI OF CHOCOLATE AND CARDAMOM

SERVES 5

Ingredients

Cardomom Mousse

50g sugar
175g cream
3 egg yolks
225g Valhona chocolate
5g cardamom powder
150g whipped cream

250g dark chocolate

Sauce

250g 70% chocolate
½ltr cold cream
(a little water in case it splits)

Method

Start making a caramel with sugar and a dash of water.

Add cream and cardamom slowly.

Bring to boil and add egg yolk, whilst stirring.

Pass onto chocolate and leave for 2 minutes to allow chocolate to melt.

Stir to combine and then fold in whipped cream.

To dress and serve

Cover ¾ of paper with chocolate.

Pipe neat line of mousse and roll with nails.

Garnish with raspberries.

042
CUCINA

Hotel Missoni Edinburgh, 1 George IV Bridge, Edinburgh EH1 1AD

0131 220 6666
www.hotelmissoni.com
cucina@hotelmissoni.com

With a prime location on the corner of George IV Bridge and the Royal Mile, just steps from Edinburgh Castle, Hotel Missoni Edinburgh is situated in the heart of Edinburgh. Positioned between the city's famous Old and New Towns, Hotel Missoni is conveniently located for many of Edinburgh's historic attractions, shopping and restaurants.

The rooms and suites enjoy stunning views over the city landmarks and the famous Royal Mile. The rooms continue the palette of black and white seen throughout and are animated with bursts of colour. Combining form and function, it has been carefully designed to meet the needs of today's modern travellers with linens chosen from the Missoni home range.

Like the great Italian family kitchen, Cucina is the heart and soul of the hotel. A collaboration between the design sensibility of Rosita Missoni and the internationally renowned chef, Giorgio Locatelli. Cucina is an expression of the simple joys, the exuberance of Italian food, Italian dining, the Italian way of life.

Mattia Camorani is head chef at Cucina. A protégé of Giorgio, Mattia hails from the famous Locatelli restaurant 'Reffetorio'. His Cucina menu presents a contemporary vision of Italian dining based on beloved, seasonal Italian ingredients.

Bar Missoni is Edinburgh's place to see and be seen. People with a passion for the subtleties of bar culture, its atmosphere, the ultimate setting against which the human drama can play itself out. Beautifully.

The unique style of the iconic Italian fashion house has redefined the design hotel to give guests a true taste of the Missoni lifestyle. Luxurious touches that really matter.

Here, life is beautiful.

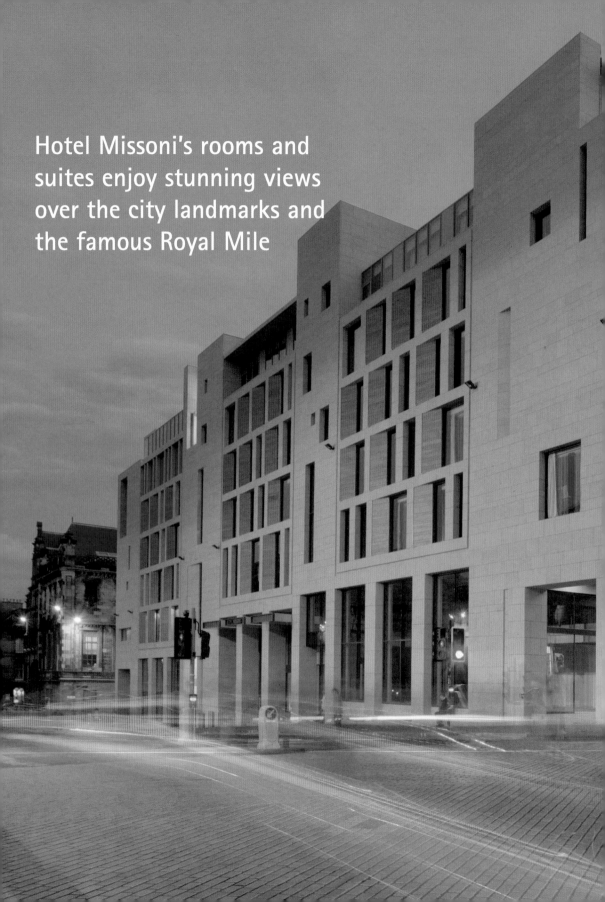

Hotel Missoni's rooms and
suites enjoy stunning views
over the city landmarks and
the famous Royal Mile

RAVIOLI OF RICOTTA AND AUBERGINES WITH CHERRY TOMATOES

SERVES 4

Ingredients

Pasta
500g of flour
3 large eggs and 2 large egg yolks
(all at room temperature)
1 beaten egg

Filling
2 skinned aubergines (ideally the pale round or
Rosa Bianca if available)
1 white onion, finely chopped
350g ricotta
150g parmesan
fresh, grated nutmeg
1 egg

Accompaniments
the skins from the aubergines
cherry tomatoes
75g butter
½ garlic clove finely chopped
toasted pine kernels

Method

For the pasta

Sieve the flour into a clean bowl and then, onto a clean surface, tip into a mound with a well to form the 'fontana di farina' (fountain of flour). Add the eggs, egg yolks and a pinch of salt.

Break the yolks and, using your hands, gradually bring the flour into the mix until it is all combined into a ball. You should knead the dough with the heel of your hand until it is springy, but still tough and all the flour is absorbed.

Wrap the dough in cling film and leave it in the fridge for 12 hours. Once the filling is ready you should roll the pasta out. If you have a pasta roller this is easiest but you can do it with a rolling pin. Roll it out and fold in on itself, repeat this several times, getting gradually thinner each time. Finally roll it to around ½ cm thick and cut into circles roughly 8cm in diameter and brush half of these with the beaten egg.

For the ricotta and aubergine filling

Cut the skinned aubergines into 1cm cubes and season with some salt in a colander to drain their liquid.

Once they are drained, deep fry the cubes a little at a time, to ensure that the excess water does not cause the oil to foam, and let them cool. Sweat the chopped onion in a pan, making sure that it softens but does not take on colour.

Mix the ricotta, aubergine, parmesan, cooked onion, nutmeg and the egg and season to taste.

Place a tablespoon full of the filling into the centre of the egg brushed pasta rounds and use the other to seal them.

Cook the ravioli al dente, in abundant salted water. Fry the garlic until soft and then add the cherry tomatoes, cut in halves, and cook until they collapse. Add the ravioli to the pan and toss with some extra butter.

For the crispy aubergine skin

Slice the skins into very thin strips and deep fry at 140°C until crispy.

To serve

Plate the pasta and the cherry tomatoes and finish with the pine kernels and the aubergine.

RACK OF INVERURIE LAMB WITH ROASTED VEGETABLES AND A BLACK OLIVE TAPENADE

SERVES 4

Ingredients

4 x 3 bone racks of lamb
1 aubergine (ideally the pale round or
Rosa Bianca if available)
2 red onions
1 red pepper
1 yellow pepper
1 courgette
12 cherry tomatoes on the vine
30ml sunflower or vegetable oil
30ml extra virgin olive oil

Tapenade

100g pitted black olives from Cerignola
5g garlic
100ml extra virgin olive oil
2 anchovies
5g of miniature capers

Method

For the tapenade

Blend all of the ingredients into a smooth paste.

For the roasted vegetable

Roast the peppers in the oven with some oil and salt for about 10 minutes or until the skin starts to come off. Remove, place them in a bowl and cover with cling film, this will make it easier to remove their skin. Once they have cooled down, remove the skin and any seeds and set aside in the fridge.

Cut the red onion and aubergines into quarters and cook them first in a hot pan to give them some colour and finish the cooking in the oven for about 10 minutes or until soft.

Slice the courgette 1cm thick and grill.

For the lamb

Preheat the oven to 200°C. Set a large, oven proof sauté pan on the hob to a medium heat with the sunflower or vegetable oil.

Season the lamb with salt and black pepper and place them in the pan. Sauté until golden (a couple of minutes on each side), making sure to keep the heat up in the pan or the meat will "boil" rather than seal.

Place the pan in the oven and cook the lamb for about 6 minutes depending on the size of the rack. This should give you medium rare but cook for longer for well done.

Remove the lamb from the oven to rest on a wire rack for around 10 minutes. Place the cherry tomatoes in the oven with some oil and salt and cook until the skin starts to break.

Place the vegetables and the lamb back in the oven for around 5 minutes.

To Serve

Slice the rack in three between the bones and spoon some of the tapenade onto each chop. Arrange on the plate with the vegetables and drizzle with the extra virgin olive oil.

TIRAMISU
SERVES 10

Ingredients

20 lady finger biscuits
enough espresso coffee to soak the lady
finger biscuits (approx. 12 shots)
20 crushed amaretti biscuits
100ml Amaretto liqueur
80g cocoa powder for dusting

Tiramisu Foam

600g mascarpone
4 eggs
113g caster sugar
40g Marsala
40g Amaretto

Method

For the tiramisu foam

Blend all of the ingredients in a large bowl until totally smooth and pass through a fine sieve.

Put the mixture in a 1 litre nitrogen siphon charged with two compressed air cartridges and leave in the fridge for a couple of hours before serving. There are other methods but this makes the lightest, most delicate of tiramisus.

To serve

Soak the lady fingers in the espresso coffee until soft. At the bottom of a wide glass arrange some of the crushed amaretti biscuit and a healthy dash of amaretto liqueur. Place half a lady finger biscuit then some of the tiramisu foam. Repeat this to the top and then sprinkle some of the crushed amaretti biscuit and finish with a dusting of cocoa powder.

052
THE DAKHIN

First Floor, 89 Candleriggs, Merchant City, Glasgow G1 1NP

0141 553 2585
www.dakhin.com

Established in 2004 Dakhin was the first authentic South Indian restaurant in Scotland. Set amidst the centre of Glasgow's Merchant city district, it offers diners a vast array of speciality dishes from India's Southern region.

One of the key distinctions between south Indian food and the more commonly available north Indian food is that rice flour is used for breads rather than wheat flour. This is particularly appealing for customers who require a gluten free diet. "Dosas" are a speciality bread which are renowned throughout South India that can be stuffed with any meat or vegetable filling and eaten with a range of tasty sauces and pickles.

The range of spices used in south Indian cuisine also varies considerably compared with other parts of India. Coconut is often used thus creating a distinctive sweet and sour flavour. Tastes range from very mild to very spicy and using the freshest of ingredients, Dakhin's highly qualified kitchen staff can prepare dishes to suit all palates.

Dakhin diners can also enjoy the views of an open plan kitchen where chefs prepare dishes and breads which are a sight to be enjoyed in their own right. The unique menu offered by Dakhin consisting of chicken, lamb, seafood and particularly vegetarian options has become a favourite amongst the discerning customer. This along with its relaxed stylish interior has ensured that Dakhin has earned its reputation as one of the best South Indian restaurants in Britain.

Dakhin diners can also enjoy the views of an open plan kitchen where chefs prepare dishes and breads which are a sight to be enjoyed in their own right

BOTATA BONDA

SERVES 10

Ingredients

500g potatoes (boiled & mash)
60g dessicated coconut powder
550ml vegetable oil
10g mustard seed oil
5g hing (Asafoetida)
5g curry leaf
10g ginger paste
10g garlic paste
5g turmeric powder
20g red chilli powder
15g fresh coriander
15g salt

Batter

150g gram flour
15ml lemon juice
15g red chilli powder
15g paprika powder
15g salt

Salad

25g iceberg lettuce
10g cabbage
10g red cabbage
10g carrot
1 lemon

Method

Heat 50ml oil in a pan and add the mustard seeds, when these begin to crackle add hing, curry leaf, ginger paste and garlic paste. Sauté for 2 minutes on a slow heat.

Add coconut powder, turmeric powder and red chilli powder along with the salt.

Add the masala to the mashed potato with coriander and mix well. Using the mixture make small balls of 25 to 30gs each

For the batter

Mix together the gram flour, lemon juice, red chilli powder, paprika powder and salt and make a smooth medium consistency batter.

To serve

Dip potato balls in gram flour then fry until golden and cooked through.

Arrange the salad - iceberg lettuce, cabbage, red cabbage, carrot and fresh coriander.

Cut the lemon into wedges and serve with fried potato balls.

VARUTHA MEEN PALUKARI

SERVES 6

Ingredients

6 whole lemon sole (300 – 350 grams each)
10g turmeric powder
20g red chilli powder
20g paprika powder
15g ginger paste
25g garlic paste
50g gram flour
1 lemon
15g salt
200ml cooking oil

Sauce

550g onion
250g tomatoes
25g fresh ginger
35g fresh garlic
10g curry leaf
20g whole cumin seed
35g whole coriander seed
35g whole dried red chilli
5g green cardamom
5g whole black peppercorn
5g clove
5g bay leaf
5g plain sonf (aniseed)
20g white sesame seed
30g poppy seed
60g dessicated coconut powder
10g turmeric powder
5g black cardamom
10g cinnamon stick
25ml tamarind sauce
75ml vegetable oil
20g salt

Garnishing

2 cucumbers (sliced)
4 tomatoes (sliced in half)
2 red onions (sliced)
6 green chillies
5g fresh coriander sprigs
20g fresh grated coconut
3 whole limes

Method

For the fish

Wash and dry the lemon sole.

Make a medium consistency batter using the lemon juice, turmeric, red chilli, paprika, ginger, garlic, gram flour and salt.

Marinate the batter on the lemon sole and leave for 20 minutes.

Pan Fry both sides on a slow heat until cooked and leave to temper.

For the sauce

Heat oil and sauté all ingredients except tomatoes and tamarind sauce until light golden brown.

Add tomatoes and hot water. Cook until the onions are softened.

Grind to a smooth paste.

Add tamarind sauce.

To serve

Serve the hot lemon sole on an oval plate. Spread some sauce on the fish and serve the balance in a separate bowl.

Decorate plate of fish with sliced cucumber, tomatoes, onions, grated coconut, split green chillies, lime and coriander sprigs.

KESREE BHATH

SERVES 6-8

Ingredients

125g semolina
200g butter ghee
350g sugar
1g saffron

Garnish

50g whole cashew nuts
30g sultanas

Method

Boil saffron in 500ml water.

Heat ghee in a pan.

Add cashew nuts and sultanas and cook for 5 minutes.

Drain and place cashew nuts and sultanas on a heated plate.

Add semolina into the same butter or ghee and pan fry on a slow heat – continuously stirring for up to 12 minutes.

When semolina starts to become golden brown add the sugar and cook for another 2-3 minutes.

Add saffron water and continue stirring ensuring smoothness of pudding.

Remove from heat and continue stirring for 3 – 4 minutes.

To serve

Serve in a bowl and sprinkle with fried cashew nuts and sultanas

THE DHABBA

44 Candleriggs, Glasgow Lanarkshire G1 1LE

0141 553 1249
www.thedhabba.com

Established in 2002, The Dhabba which means "diner" in Punjabi, prides itself in providing authentic North Indian cuisine. Only the freshest ingredients sourced from Scotland and spices from India are used to prepare the vast array of dishes available. The menu contains dishes that would be commonly found in restaurants throughout Northern India. Six different base sauces are used to create the menu, all of which offer a very distinct flavour and are only suited to particular meat, seafood or vegetable dishes. The Dhabba has never used any food colouring products however manages to offer naturally colourful and flavoursome food, all of which is created with careful preparation. It was one of the first Indian restaurants in Scotland to recruit high calibre professional chefs from India, some of whom have cooked for presidents, government officials and celebrities on an individual basis in India.

The Dhabba specialises in Dum Pukht dishes which originate from the days of the 'Nawabs of India' – rulers of the Northern provinces during the 18th century. 'Dum Pukht' means 'to breathe' and 'to cook'. What makes this cuisine special is that the food, sealed in a dish, is cooked in its own juices and retains all its natural flavours and aromas.

Located in the heart of the Merchant City of Glasgow, The Dhabba is very well suited for tourists and business people visiting. It has also welcomed a very regular customer base from people who reside across the city as a whole. The interior has unique combination of traditional and contemporary design. With a capacity of 100, the Dhabba caters for large group bookings or intimate dinners with no dress code restrictions.

Located in the heart of the Merchant City of Glasgow, The Dhabba is very well suited for tourists and business people visiting. It has also welcomed a very regular customer base from people who reside across the city as a whole

MILI JULI SABZI SEEKH

SERVES 6-8

Ingredients

10 medium button mushrooms
1 large potato
1 medium cauliflower
1 medium green pepper
1 medium red pepper
½ medium onion
15g salt
½ medium lemon
½ tea spoon turmeric powder

Marinade

250g full fat yogurt
50g mustard oil
20g ginger paste
25g garlic paste
25g tandoori masala powder
20g garam masala powder
15g red chilli powder
15g paprika powder
15g coriander powder
15g cumin powder
10g kasoori methi
15g salt

Garnish

25g Iceberg lettuce
10g fresh coriander
10g cabbage
10g red cabbage
10g carrot
1 lemon
5g chat masala

Method

Peel and cut the potato into 12 pieces.

Separate florettes from cauliflower.

Cut each pepper into 6 pieces.

Chop the onion into large pieces.

Boil water with salt, lemon and turmeric powder

Half boil the cauliflower. Remove them from the water then boil potatoes in the same water until half cooked.

For the marinade

Mix all ingredients in a large bowl and whisk for 3 to 4 minutes.

Leave marinating for 15 to 20 minutes.

Mix all the prepared vegetables in marinade and leave for 10 minutes.

Skewer vegetables on an iron rod and cook in tandoor/ barbecue for 5 to 6 minutes until they start browning.

To serve

Mix the shredded Iceberg lettuce, cabbage, carrot and half of the coriander with half of the chat masala.

Put half of the salad in the centre of large plate and the other half spread around the plate.

Arrange the cooked vegetables on the plate and sprinkle with coriander and chat masala.

Arrange lemon wedges and serve.

TANDOORI MACHI

SERVES 4

Ingredients

4 Black Bream (350gm)
2 lemons

First marination

80ml mustard oil
20ml lemon juice
30gm ginger garlic paste
20gm red chilli powder
20gm paprika powder
20gm coriander powder
cumin powder 20gm
40gm garam masala powder
25gm salt
10gm Ajwain
10gm Kasoori Meithei

Second marination

120gm yoghur
40ml mustard oil
30gm red chilli powder
30gm paprika powder
30gm coriander powder
30gm cumin powde
30gm salt
10gm Kasoori Meithei

Makai Mutter Chawal

250gm basmati rice
12gm salt
40gm sweetcorn
60gm green peas
50gm butter
15gm coriander

Tadka

30ml oil
7gm whole jeera
4gm heeng (asfotida)
7gm garlic (chopped)
1 onion (chopped)
2 tomato (chopped)
7gm green chilli (chopped)
10gm ginger (chopped)
10gm coriander (chopped)

Method

For the bream

Clean wash and make ³/₄ cuts on bream from both side.

Leave in cold water with ¹/₂ lemon juice for 10 minute.

Remove from water and dry fish.

Mix all ingredient from first marination and rub on fish on both sides and leave for 45 minutes.

Mix all ingredients from second marination and mix with fish and leave for another 45 minutes.

Cook on barbeque or tandoor.

Serve hot on sizzler with salad and lemon.

For the Makai Mutter Chawal

Clean wash and soak rice for 1 hour .

Heat butter in a heavy pan put rice without water and fry for 2 to 3 minutes on slow heat.

Put water, salt and cook on high flame till rice ³/₄ done.

slow heat put green peas and sweet corn cover and cook for another ³/₄ minute.

Mix coriander and serve.

For the tadka

Heat oil in a heavy pan, add cumin seed and crackle it, add heeng and cook for 20 seconds.

Add garlic and onion and cook until golden brown.

Add tomato, chilli and ginger cook until mashed.

Now pour dal on tomato masala and cook until dal is mashed.

Add coriander and mix well and serve.

CHAWAL KI KHEER

SERVES 6-8

Ingredients

1 litre full fat milk
75g Basmati rice
100g condensed milk
40g pure butter ghee
50g sugar
30g sultanas
¼ tea spoon green cardamom powder

Garnish

50g whole cashew nuts

Method

Wash and soak the rice for 30 minutes.

Wash and soak sultanas in luke warm water.

Boil milk with condensed milk and continue on a slow heat

Heat butter ghee in a separate pan and fry the cashew nuts until golden brown.

Place cashew nuts on a heated plate for garnish.

Within the same ghee put soaked rice and fry for 4 to 5 minutes at slow heat.

Put rice into boiling milk with ghee and continue cooking until rice starts to soften and break.

Add cardamom powder and remove from heat.

Add the sultanas and sugar and mix well.

Serve topped with fried cashew nuts.

You can enjoy this dessert chilled or luke warm.

072 DALHOUSIE CASTLE

Bonnyrigg, Edinburgh EH19 3JB

01875 820 153
www.dalhousiecastle.co.uk

When numerous AA Rosettes are combined with the most archetypal of Scottish castle experience it's easy to see why Dalhousie Castle's Dungeon restaurant has become one of the most popular gastronomic venues in Scotland.

Head Chef, Francois Giraud's modern European style is combined with Scottish influences to produce cuisine which will excite and tantalise the palate. Francois sources the finest, freshest, locally sourced ingredients which are heavily influenced by seasonality. Indeed the most succulent lamb available is sourced from just down the road in fact!

Suits of armour and medieval paraphernalia are situated elegantly within the Dungeon dining room. Lit by candlelight you cannot help but become romantically entwined with this unique venue. The hotel also has "The Orangery Restaurant" which offers a relaxed addition to the hotel and award winning spa with enchanting views overlooking the River South Esk. Part of the von Essen collection of hotels which contains the most Michelin stars and AA Rosettes of any hotel group in the UK, Dalhousie Castle's magical Scottish experience is sure to last long in the memory.

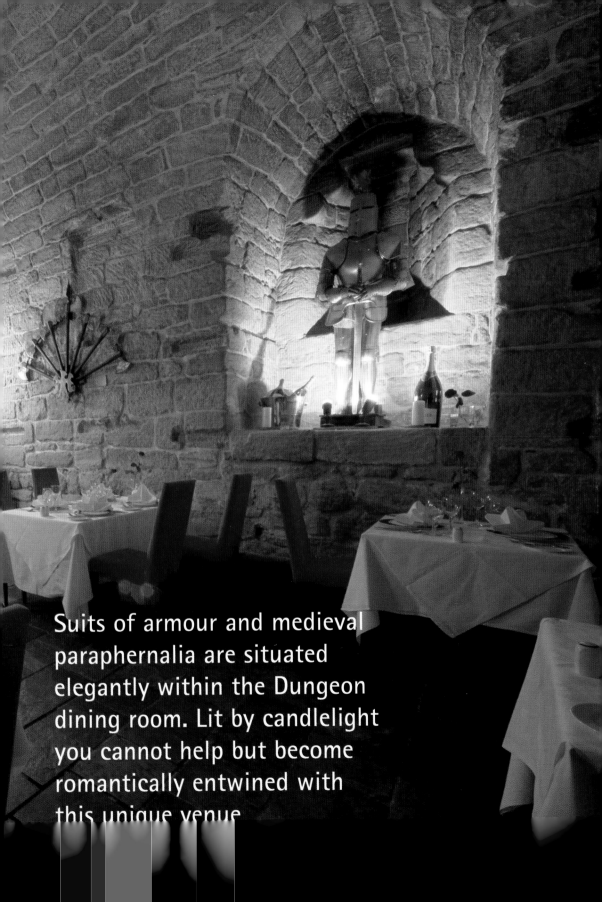

Suits of armour and medieval paraphernalia are situated elegantly within the Dungeon dining room. Lit by candlelight you cannot help but become romantically entwined with this unique venue.

LOBSTER AND SAFFRON TORTELLINI WITH LOBSTER CREAM

SERVES 6

Ingredients

Pancetta and Salad

1 large or two small lobsters
2 carrots
2 onions
4 sticks of celery
2 clove of garlic
1 tbsp of plain flour and tomato paste
125ml dbl cream

Pasta

1 egg + 4 yolks
250g "00" flour
1 tbl spoon of olive oil
2g saffron

Parsnip Purée

300g parsnips
1 vanilla bean
125ml dbl cream

Lobster filling

1 pkt tarragon
1 shallot
1 lime
olive oil
1 egg yolk

Method

For the lobster and lobster cream

Boil lobsters in pan (between 9 to 12 minutes size dependant) with half the veg.

Cool then peel keeping the shells, body and some of the lobster stock for the lobster cream. In a hot pan fry the rest of the veg with some oil then add shells allow to colour until brown then add tomato paste and flour and allow to cook out then add a splash of brandy, flambé then add stock (enough to cover shells) and 125ml of cream and reduce by half then pass stock through fine sieve.

For the pasta

Infuse saffron in a couple of teaspoons of warm water. Place flour in food processor or mixing bowl, add a teaspoon of salt olive oil and saffron. When this is mixing add the egg, then yolks one by one. The mix should come together like large crumbs, if not add a little more yolk, then work by hand for another couple of minutes. It should have a slight yellow tint and be fairly stiff to touch. Allow to rest wrapped in cling film.

For the filling

Finely dice lobster making sure the entrail has been taken out! Add shallot finely chopped and half the packet of tarragon, zest of lime, and olive oil to bind and season.

Roll out paste to finest setting, cut into rings with largest cutter, fill with lobster (about 1 good teaspoon), brush the rim with egg yolk fold over then pinch opposite side. Sit flat on a floured plate and leave to firm up (1 hour in fridge).

For the parsnip purée

Peel and dice parsnips, place in a pan with some butter, shallots and the split vanilla bean. Allow to colour gently then cover with water and cream. Cook until soft then purée.

Grill pancetta until crisp.

FILLET OF BEEF WITH RED WINE REDUCTION AND BONE MARROW CROQUETTES, SCOTTISH GIROLLES, SPINACH AND POTATO STACK

SERVES 6

Ingredients

6 x 200 – 225g fillet of beef

The Sauce

3 mushrooms
2 shallots
200ml red wine (one with strong tannins)
500ml meat stock (good quality)

The Girolles

300g girolles
2 shallots
1 packet of tarragon

Spinach Purée

I packet of baby leaf spinach
1 clove of garlic

Bone Marrow

6 nice pieces of bone marrow
1 egg
1 packet of panko bread crumbs
1 packet of parsley
100ml milk
100g plain flour

Potato stack

6 large potatoes
2 packet of butter
6 cocktail sticks

Method

For potato stack

Shape potatoes into rounds using cutter, thinly slice then stack 5-6cm high, keeping them in line. Stick a cocktail stick through the middle, place in a pan of clarified butter then cook for 20 minutes in the oven at 180°C. Then leave in butter for a further 10 minutes before lifting them out, making sure the cocktail stick is still in place. Allow to rest. When potato is on plate pullout the cocktail stick before serving!!.

For the sauce

Sweat mushrooms, sliced shallot, bay leaf and wine in a pan. Reduce by half then add stock, allow to reduce again by half then strain through sieve.

For the spinach purée

Fry garlic in a hot pan with some butter add spinach and a pinch of salt. Allow to wilt then purée in a blender

For the bone marrow

In three separate bowls - 1 with flour the other with egg beaten with milk and a little salt and pepper. The last with panko crumbs and chopped parsley. Place the marrow firstly in flour then egg wash and lastly crumbs and repeat. Allow to rest in fridge or even better freeze.

To cook

Either fry in butter then oven for a minute or two, or in a chip fryer.

Fry the fillets in a pan with some butter (to the way you like them).

For the Girolles

In the pan, where the fillets were cooking, fry the girolles making sure the pan is as hot as possible without burning the sugars from the meat. Then add the shallots and lastly just before serving chopped tarragon.

WHITE CHOCOLATE AND RASPBERRY DESSERT, MOUSSE, BONBON, AND SOUP

SERVES 6

Ingredients

Mousse

1 punnet of raspberries
300g white chocolate
300ml double cream

Raspberry Soup

2 punnets of raspberries
1 lime
1 vanilla pod
150g caster sugar
100ml water

Clotted Cream Foam

100g sugar syrup
100g clotted cream

For the bon bons

Freeze dried raspberries
200g white chocolate
200ml cream

Coulis

2 punnets of raspberries
100ml water
100g caster sugar

A few fresh raspberries to garnish

Method

For the mousse

Melt chocolate, then add 100ml of double cream to chill. Whisk rest of cream adding raspberries near the end, gently fold in chocolate when cool. Set in moulds in freezer.

For the soup

In a bowl place raspberries, water, sugar, lime zest, and split vanilla pod, cover with cling film and sit on a pan of boiling water and cook for an hour. Then leave to infuse over night, strain juice through fine sieve.

For the foam

Simply mix clotted cream and syrup over a mild heat then allow to cool. To froth up simple use a stick blender.

For the bonbons

Melt chocolate, add freeze dried raspberries to taste (keeping some back to roll the bonbons in at the end), and then 50ml of cream to cool. Whisk 150g of cream, then fold in. When chocolate is cool. place in container in fridge until the mix has set. Using a hot spoon, scoop out the chocolate into little clusters then roll in some of the raspberry powder.

For the coulis

Place all ingredients in pan and cook, blend and reduce until you have the desired consistency not forgetting that it will thicken when cold.

082
THE DINING ROOM

28 Queen Street, Edinburgh EH2 1JX

0131 220 2044
www.thediningroomedinburgh.co.uk
www.smws.co.uk

The Dining Room opened in 2004 as part of The Scotch Malt Whisky Society's beautifully restored Georgian town house at 28 Queen Street. The Society had been looking to unleash the creative spirit and natural talent of executive chef James Freeman who had impressed members for many years at their Leith venue, The Vaults. James continued to build on his reputation and helped develop The Dining Room as one of the main fine dining destinations in the capital.

"Although the restaurant is open to non-members, feedback from regular members gave us the confidence to build our 'crafted' style - emphasising natural, honest cooking with simple elegance. Broadly speaking our cooking style is modern European, built upon a firm respect for sound technique and understanding the science behind our methods. Crucially, using good marriages of flavour allows ingredients to really shine together. Complimentary combinations and contrasting texture is where the magic is."

A collective approach is encouraged, valuing contributions and critique from customers, waiters and chefs alike. This collaboration, along with good sourcing, regular dish changes as seasons turn, and allowing spontaneity all help keep the menu alive. We were delighted when the Michelin 2010 guide reviewed us as having 'modern accomplished cooking'. The main thing is we like to keep it fun and lighthearted. It's just cooking - and we intend to enjoy it."

The Dining Room's personable, well-trained staff are more than capable to recommend a dram with any of the exquisite dishes. SMWS is home to the world's widest selection of single cask, single malt whiskies.

STEAMED COURGETTE FLOWER WITH SCALLOPS, BASIL NAGE

SERVES 4

Ingredients

Nage

1ltr water
35ml white wine vinegar
130ml white wine
dice of celery, onion, leek and fennel
basil stalks
100ml double cream

Mousse

6 scallops
1 egg white
100ml double cream
10 basil leaves finely sliced

To serve

4 courgette flowers
4 plum tomato insides
12 scallops halved
small basil leaves

Method

Courgettes, basil and scallops are a great match as the flavours complement so well. It is perfect as a light, summery hors d'oeuvre. Use plenty of the basil nage to keep it moist and 'soupy'.

For the nage

Place all liquids except cream into a pan. Add a small dice of the vegetables until reaching the top of the liquid. Simmer for 40 minutes. Pass through a sieve, and reduce the liquid to 200mls. Add the double cream and bubble for 30 seconds. Remove from heat and set aside.

For the mousse

Whiz the cleaned scallops in a blender with the egg white. Fold in the double cream, basil and seasoning. Chill, and then pipe into the courgette flowers.

To serve

Steam the courgette flowers for 5 minutes. Scoop the seeds from the tomatoes and season. Mark the scallops in a hot grill pan on the cut side only for 90 seconds. Arrange the above ingredients in wide bowls. Heat the sauce, whisking thoroughly before pouring generously around and garnish with small basil leaves.

ROSÉ VEAL WITH SWEETBREADS, WHITE PORT, SAGE AND PARMESAN

SERVES 4

Method

The crusted veal braise and polenta can be prepared in advance to allow easy serving.

For the veal with parmesan and sage crust

First strain the veal from the braising liquor. Reduce the liquor down to sauce consistency and add white port to taste. Add a touch of this sauce to the veal braise and season, reserving the remainder. Whizz the bread, butter and parmesan in a blender, adding the sage once smooth. Form the braised veal in to 4 rounds on a baking tray placing discs of crust on top and refrigerate.

To make the polenta

Heat the chicken stock until bubbling and whisk in the polenta until thick. Change to stirring with a spatula, and cook out with cream until very smooth, adding more liquid if necessary. When ready to serve, beat in parmesan until soft and glossy and season.

To serve

Place the braised veal and crust in the oven for 10 minutes. Dust the raw sweetbreads lightly in seasoned flour and sizzle in hot oil for 8 minutes. Sear the veal fillet in oil on both sides for 90 seconds, then rest. Heat the polenta gently, and meanwhile sauté the broadbeans and girolles in a little butter and water for a couple of minutes. Arrange the items on the plate, slicing the veal fillets in two, and reheating the sauce with more sliced sage to finish.

Ingredients

Parmesan veal crust

400g braised veal in stock
4 slices white bread
50g butter
25g parmesan
8 sage leaves sliced

Soft polenta

100g polenta
100ml chicken stock
100ml double cream
30g parmesan

To serve

4 x 150g veal fillet
200g broadbeans
4 x 50g sweetbreads
200g girolles
white port

POACHED MOUNTAIN PEACH, LEMON THYME CURD, RASPBERRY RIPPLE PARFAIT

SERVES 4

Ingredients

Poached peaches

4 mountain peaches
250ml champagne
250ml water
250g caster sugar
1/2 vanilla pod split
zest of 1 lemon

Lemon Thyme Curd

zest and juice of 3 lemons
100g chilled unsalted butter
200g caster sugar
3 free range eggs
1 tbsp lemon thyme leaves

Raspberry Ripple Parfait

100ml raspberry purée
1/2 sheet gelatine in cold water
3 eggs separated
125ml double cream
125g clotted cream
90g caster sugar
1/2 vanilla pod

To serve

raspberry purée
fresh raspberries

Method

For the peaches

Remove the stones using an apple corer. Bring the remaining ingredients to a simmer and poach the fruit covered in a small pan for 20 minutes. Remove peaches, allow to cool slightly and peel carefully. Reserve the poaching liquor.

In a small saucepan, bring the zest, juice, thyme leaves and half the sugar to the boil. Meanwhile, whisk the remaining sugar and eggs in a metal bowl until pale. Pour the boiling lemon stock into the bowl and whisk thoroughly. Return to the pan, and whisk simmering over a medium heat until thickened. Remove from the heat and whisk in the cold butter gradually until smooth. Refrigerate.

For the parfait

Gently warm 1/4 of the purée and whisk in the softened gelatine. Add the remaining purée and set aside. Whisk both creams and vanilla until semi-whipped. Whisk the egg yolks and half the sugar until light and creamy and gently fold in the cream mixture.

Now beat the egg whites in a clean metal bowl until doubled in volume. Sprinkle the remaining sugar gradually until reaching a shiny meringue. Fold the meringue in to the cream mixture in batches until even. Swirl the raspberry purée into the parfait mix creating the ripple and freeze in the mould of your choice for 3 hours.

To serve

Glaze the peaches with reduced poaching liquor and garnish with the curd, parfait raspberries and any leftover purée.

092
THE FORTH FLOOR RESTAURANT
AT HARVEY NICHOLS

30-34 St Andrew Square, Edinburgh EH2 2AD

0131 524 8388
www.harveynichols.com

Stuart Muir Executive Chef at the Forth Floor Restaurant has been with Harvey Nichols since opening in August 2002 where he has earned a reputation for producing constantly exciting dishes created from the very best, Scottish produce.

Stuart acquired his love of cooking from his parents. His father fishing and shooting on the local rivers and moors and his mother preparing and cooking the fresh produce, Stuart has been cooking ever since.

He won his Michelin Star and 3AA rosettes at the age of 22 while he was the Head Chef at Knockinaam Lodge. Stuart was the youngest chef to win this prestigious accolade in Scotland.

After a brief spell travelling the world gaining a wealth of experience from a number of other Michelin Star Chefs he went on to the Balmoral Edinburgh to be chef at Number One and Hadrian's.

From here Stuart went to be Executive Chef at the famous Old Course Hotel in St Andrews.

He then decided to return to Edinburgh to launch the award winning Forth Floor Restaurant at Harvey Nichols.

Stuart, recognised as one of the twelve best chefs in Scotland by the Scottish Chef's association 2006 – uses a selection of locally sourced produce to create dishes that match modern flavours with classical technique.

Executive Chef Stuart Muir, has earned a reputation for producing constantly exciting dishes created from the very best Scottish produce

ROSE VEAL FILLET WRAPPED IN AYRSHIRE BACON WITH SOUSED SHALLOTS, ROASTED HAZELNUTS, CELERIAC PURÉE AND FRIED QUAIL EGG

SERVES 4

Ingredients

150g Ayrshire bacon
750g rose veal fillet
1 banana shallot
50g caster sugar
50ml white wine vinegar (any clear vinegar will do)
50g whole hazelnuts
1 dessert spoon treacle
1 small celeriac
150ml double cream
1 fennel bulb
250g picked spinach
4 quail eggs (optional)
splash hazelnut oil
beef stock ready to serve

Method

Check that veal doesn't have any obvious fat and remove if present.

Roll 2 layers of cling film on a bench surface, layer bacon just overlapping and place veal on top. Season with salt and pepper and roll in cling film ensuring cling film is not under the bacon.

Portion into 4 and place in fridge.

Finely dice 1 shallot and cook in pan with sugar and vinegar until all the liquid evaporates.

Peel the celeriac and dice. Cook in cream until very soft and blend using extra cream if required.

Gently grill the hazelnuts until just starting to colour, then coat in treacle while still hot.

Thinly slice fennel 4 times.

Open quail eggs and place in small separate cups.

Pan fry the veal fillet sealing the bacon where it over laps first to stop it from opening.

Once every side is coloured place on a tray and in the oven at 180ºC for 8-10 minutes. Allow 5-10 minutes for resting the veal after cooking.

While veal is cooking reheat the celeriac purée and shallots separately and leave hot at side of stove.

Blanch the fennel slices in seasoned water until cooked. In the same water blanch spinach and dry off.

Place a generous spoon of celeriac purée on a plate and spread across the plate with the back of the spoon, place fennel on top and then the veal on top of the fennel, place spinach beside veal, spoon the shallots on to the veal.

Pan fry the quail eggs gently in a sauce pan until white of egg is cooked.

To serve

Place quail egg on top of veal beside the shallots and sprinkle the hazelnuts over the outer edge of the plate

Drizzle hazelnut oil and beef stock around the plate and serve.

POACHED ATLANTIC HALIBUT WITH SUMMER VEGETABLES, CHERVIL AND ANISEED NAGE, LOCH ETIVE OYSTERS AND BRAISED CABBAGE

SERVES 4

Ingredients

4 portions Atlantic halibut at roughly 200g each

For the sauce

2kg fish bones
1 carrot
1 fennel
1 onion
1 leek
2 cloves garlic
2 bay leaves
2 star anise
200ml white wine
Small bunch picked chervil
(keep the stalks as well).

For the garnish

1 packet baby carrots
1 packet baby fennel
1 packet baby leeks
8 new potatoes
1 small savoy or spring cabbage
8 oysters

Method

Wash fish bones, peel and roughly chop all veg for sauce ingredients.

Sweat off all the sauce veg, bay leaves, star anise and chervil stalks in a large sauce pan without letting it brown.

Add the white wine and reduce until the liquid has almost gone.

Add fish bones and cover with water. Simmer for 20 minutes then pass through a fine sieve.

Separate the sauce into 2 pans and reduce 1 of them by 3/4.

Scrub baby carrots, top and tail the baby leeks and fennel and cut to approximately the same size. Peel the new potatoes and thinly slice the cabbage.

Open oysters, remove from shell and place in a small bowl.

Boil potatoes in water, 5 minutes before they are ready in a separate pot of water cook the baby veg by adding the carrots first.

4 minutes later add the fennel and leeks then cook for a further 2 minutes.

Drain off the potatoes and baby veg then season with salt and pepper.

Braise cabbage in water for a few minutes then strain and season.

Now place the halibut portions in the large pot of simmering sauce and simmer for 3 -4 minutes depending on thickness of halibut and remove from pot ready to serve.

To serve

Plate up in 4 bowls, adding the braised cabbage with baby veg and potatoes around it; place the cooked halibut on top of the cabbage.

In the smaller pot of reduced sauce add the chopped chervil and oysters, pour over each halibut and serve immediately.

STRAWBERRY DISH

SERVES 4

Ingredients

Clotted Cream Panna Cotta

150ml clotted cream
25g caster sugar
70ml milk
1 leaf gelatin
5ml vanilla essence

Strawberry Jelly

170g strawberries puréed and strained
20g caster sugar
50ml water
2 leaves gelatin
100ml cold water

Caramel for Dipped Strawberries

240ml cold water
455g caster sugar
100ml glucose
4 strawberries
4 wooden skewers

Method

For the clotted cream panna cotta

Soak the gelatin in cold water to soften.

In a pan over a low heat mix the milk and sugar until the sugar dissolves.

Remove the gelatin from the cold water and add to the warm milk. Mixing well to ensure the gelatin is fully dissolved.

Mix in the clotted cream and vanilla essence.

Pour into serving dishes and refrigerate

For the strawberry jelly

Soak gelatin in cold water until soft.

Bring sugar and water to a boil. Boil for 4 minutes. Add gelatin and strawberry purée.

Pour into serving dishes and refrigerate.

For the caramel

Prepare a bowl of cold water large enough to fit the pan and set aside. Also place a clean pastry brush in a cup of water to have on hand to wash down the sides of the pan.

Take one skewer and slide through each top of the strawberry just under the stem.

Place sugar, water and glucose in a stainless steel pan.

Bring to a boil stirring constantly to dissolve the sugar. Remove any foam that accumulates.

Brush the sides of the pan with the pastry brush dipped in water. Continue this process as long as you can see sugar crystals alongside the pan.

Once the sugar begins to change to a light golden colour it will turn quickly to golden brown. Just as the sugar starts to turn golden brown, remove the pan from the stove and place in the bowl of cold water. Take extra caution when placing into the water as a drop of water will cause the sugar to react fiercely.

Hold the pan in the water until the bubbles have subsided. Remove from the water and dry the bottom of the pan.

Place a wooden spoon on a heat resistant surface, and place the pan on the wooden spoon to slant the syrup to one side.

Dip each strawberry and rest on a piece of silicone paper (do not use greaseproof).

Do not refrigerate as this will melt the sugar.

102
GLENAPP CASTLE

Ballantrae, Ayrshire KA26 0NZ

01465 831212
www.glenappcastle.com

Glenapp Castle was built in 1870 - a strikingly beautiful example of the Scottish Baronial style of architecture. The Castle was designed by the celebrated architect David Bryce for Mr James Hunter, the Deputy Lord Lieutenant of Ayrshire. The castle's mellow sandstone battlements are topped by soaring turrets and towers, earning Glenapp a rightful place as one of the most romantic castles in Scotland. Following a full restoration and refurbishment by owners Graham and Fay Cowan, the castle was opened as a luxury country house in 2000. Head Chef Adam Stokes came to Glenapp 3 years ago after seven years at Hambleton Hall on Rutland Water in Leicestershire. His modern British style, using classic marriages of flavours coupled with inventive twists creates spectacular dishes - a delight to all the senses. Adam and his team have already been awarded numerous accolades including 3AA Rosettes and the EatScotland Gold Award. Adam puts this down to producing exciting, fun and accurate dishes day in, day out.

Each evening the Castle serves a six course gourmet menu utilising the best fresh and seasonal local ingredients. Adam has revelled in the fact that there are so many of the country's finest ingredients available nearby. Lobster and crab from Ballantrae Bay, beef and lamb from a farm just around the corner, wonderful cheeses from around Scotland as well as fruit, vegetables and herbs from our own walled garden and glasshouses.

Each evening the castle serves a six course gourmet menu utilising the best fresh and seasonal local ingredients

SMOKED AYRSHIRE HAM HOCK AND FOIE GRAS TERRINE WITH 'PICCALILLI' FLAVOURS AND ROASTED HAZELNUT DRESSING

SERVES 4

Ingredients

Terrine

2 smoked ham hocks
1 shallot
3 sprigs parsley
100g chicken stock
200g cooked foie gras
50g pistachio nuts
100g bouillon
50g orange juice
50g madeira
5 leaves gelatine
8 slices Parma ham

Dressing

1 egg yolk
100ml of good quality roasted hazelnut oil

Piccalilli

8 florets of curried cauliflower
4 caramelised grelot onions
1 pickled dill cucumber
4 green beans

Garnish

micro watercress sprigs

Method

For the terrine

Place the ham hocks, shallot and parsley in a vacuum pack bag with stock. Seal and cook in water at 82°C for 16 hours, cool and pick meat from bone. Roll foie gras into cylinders and cool. Boil bouillon, orange juice and Madeira for two minutes, soak gelatine in water till soft add to bouillon and set aside. Line a terrine mould with cling film and place slices of Parma ham on the sides of the mould, continue by placing the ham, foie gras, cooked parsley and pistachio nuts decoratively inside the mould, coating with bouillon jelly mix until full. Fold the overlapping Parma ham on top and wrap tightly in cling film, press and place in fridge overnight.

To serve

Slice terrine, garnish with piccalilli and micro watercress sprigs.

For the Dressing

Place egg yolk in a food processor and add oil slowly until you have a thick emulsion, then add a tablespoon of water.

SEARED LOIN OF LAMB WITH CRISPY CAPERS AND HERB BOUDIN

SERVES 4

Ingredients

Lamb

1 double best end of spring lamb
10ml olive oil
1 sprig of rosemary
1 clove of garlic

Lamb Shank Boudin

1 cooked lamb shank
700g chicken
700ml double cream
1 yolk
100g dried breadcrumbs
20ml olive oil
200g chopped parsley, chervil, chives
3g salt

Garnish

30 capers

Method

For the lamb

Bone out best end and trim fat and sinews off loin. Place lamb loin, oil, rosemary and garlic in a vacuum pack bag and cook at 63°C for 45 minutes.

For the Boudin

Purée chicken, add egg yolk, then add cream slowly and reserve. Blitz breadcrumbs, olive oil, herbs and salt until you have fine green bread crumbs. Pick the meat off the lamb shank bone and place in a bowl. Add 3 tablespoons of chicken mousse mix then roll in cling film and tie with string. Cook for 3 minutes in boiling water. Release from cling film and roll in breadcrumbs. Grill gently until golden brown.

For the garnish

Deep fry capers until they open.

To serve

Place lamb in hot pan to colour the outside. Slice and garnish with Scottish girolles and chervil.

MILK CHOCOLATE AND GRAND MARNIER MOUSSE WITH ORANGE CURD ICE CREAM

SERVES 4

Method

For the chocolate case

Cut strips of acetate to 18cm long. Place a small spoonful of the melted dark chocolate onto the acetate and run the wood graining tool along the length. Allow this to cool at 11°C for 12 minutes. Place a spoonful of the melted white chocolate onto the grained acetate and smooth with a palette knife. Shape acetate into a 4cm diameter round mould to create a cylinder. Cool at around 11°C for 12 minutes.

For the mousse

Bring milk to the boil and add Grand Marnier. Bring to boil again and add to the yolks. Whisk until pale and fluffy. Add to chocolate and stir. Finally add the cream and pour into the chocolate moulds to set overnight.

For the ice cream

In a Bain-Marie melt the butter adding the orange zest and orange juice. Infuse the vanilla pod with whipping cream over heat. Whisk the caster sugar with 20g of egg yolk until fluffy. Add the sugar and egg mixture to the melted butter. Whisk the remaining 14g of egg yolks into the whipping cream and pass through muslin. Add two mixtures together and churn in ice cream machine.

To serve

Carefully peel the acetate from the chocolate cylinder and place in middle of the plate. Scoop ice cream on top of mousse and garnish with candied orange zest

Ingredients

Chocolate

50g dark 70% chocolate melted
100g white chocolate melted
50mm wide acetate strips

Mousse

100g milk chocolate melted
40g egg yolk
34g milk
8ml Grand Marnier
100g whipping cream (whipped until soft)

Orange Curd Ice Cream

50g caster sugar
34g egg yolk
50g butter
1 orange zest
50g orange juice
73g whipping cream
½ vanilla pod

Garnish

candied orange zest

112
THE GRILL ROOM AT THE SQUARE

29 Royal Exchange Square, Glasgow G1 3AJ

0141 225 5615
www.thegrillroomglasgow.com

Glasgow's premier steakhouse, The Grill Room at The Square has been committed to providing outstanding hospitality and serving the best Scottish steaks since 2006.

Head Chef David Friel has been the innovation behind the success of The Grill Room and has maintained the high standards of produce and service through the teams' hard work and determination.

The prime steaks are dry-aged for tenderness and flavour and are hand cut on the premises daily.

The steaks are cooked on an open charcoaled grill and seasoned with a secret recipe seasoning. To show the quality of our beef our steaks are presented very simply, with sides served in sharing pots.

Offering a choice of sharing steaks and a variety of different cuts such as the Bone-in Rib-eye, our multi award winning Fillet, Chateaubriand and our Porterhouse Steak... All served with customer's choice of sauce and side orders.

The front of house staff are fully trained on the Scottish produce prepared within the Grill Room Kitchen and this information is passed on to our customers daily.

The stunning surroundings and excellent service are designed to provide you with a truly memorable steakhouse experience.

The Grill Room are very proud to have won the Restaurant Magazine UK's Best Steak & Chips in 2007 as well as the Daily Record's Hot Plate Award in 2008 and The Variety Awards Best New Chef in 2009. We are listed in the Michelin Guide 2010, whilst also being Members of the Scotch Beef Club, Winners of Open Table's 'Dinners Choice Award 2009/2010' and winners of 'Visit Scotland' Silver Award 2010/2011.

Head Chef David Friel has been the innovation behind the success of The Grill Room and has maintained the high standards of produce and service through the teams' hard work and determination

STORNOWAY BLACK PUDDING AND WEST COAST SCALLOPS WITH CAULIFLOWER PURÉE, QUAILS EGGS AND CRISPY PANCETTA

SERVES 1

Ingredients

3 small discs of Stornoway black pudding
3 scallops
drizzle of walnut oil
50g cauliflower
200ml milk
2 quail's eggs
3 pieces of thin crisp pancetta pieces
seasoning
tomato dressing
herb oil
micro herbs

Method

Cook the quail's eggs, peel then half and set aside.

Cook the cauliflower in the milk till tender, drain and purée, season to taste and set aside.

Grill the black pudding until heated through.

Roast the scallops in a hot pan with a little walnut oil and season.

Dress the plate with the herb oil, tomato dressing and the micro herbs.

Arrange the black pudding with the scallop on top, then add the cauliflower purée on top and finally the quails eggs and pancetta.

BONE IN RIB OF SCOTCH BEEF WITH PEPPERCORN SAUCE AND CHUNKY CHIPS

SERVES 1

Ingredients

1 x 450g bone in rib eye steak
1 Portobello mushroom
1 organic tomato
shallot salt
olive oil
6 chunky cut Maris Piper potato chips
2ltr beef dripping or vegetable oil

Peppercorn sauce

28g shallots finely diced
28g crushed dried green peppercorns
25ml brandy
14g unsalted butter
25ml veal or beef jus
25ml double cream

Method

For the chips

Blanch the chips in beef dripping at 130°C for 12 minutes then set aside.

Finish the chips at 180°C till crisp golden and cooked through.

For the sauce

Melt the butter till foaming, add shallots and cook without colour until shiny, add peppercorns and cook for a few seconds, add brandy and flambé, add the jus and reduce a little, add cream and season to taste and set aside.

For the garnish

Drizzle the mushroom with a little olive oil and season.

Blanch, peel and dip the tomato in the shallot salt, grill the tomato and mushroom together when required.

For the steak

Take the steak out of the fridge a good half hour before cooking.

Baste it in a little olive oil and seasoning then cook on the grill to your preferred cooking degree. Allow to rest for 5 minutes after cooking.

To serve

Arrange neatly.

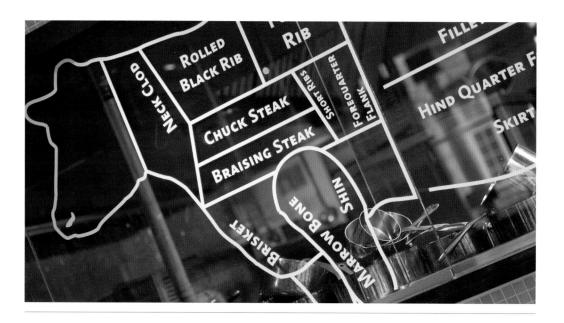

APPLE TART TATIN

SERVES 1

Ingredients

1 Braeburn apple
good quality butter puff pastry
25g caster sugar
25g unsalted butter
good quality vanilla ice cream

Caramel Sauce

1 tin condensed milk

Caramel Run Out

150g caster sugar
10g glucose syrup
water

Method

For the caramel run out

Put sugar and glucose in a pan with just enough water to cover the sugar.

Put on a high heat.

When it starts to boil brush down the inside of the pan with cold water, this stops the sugar from crystallising.

Continue brushing as you go.

Using a sugar thermometer bring the temperature up to 155°C.

Take off the stove and cool the pan in some cold water.

Using a spoon drizzle the caramel over greaseproof paper making circular shapes.

Once cold and set store in an air tight container until ready to use.

For the caramel sauce

Place the unopened tin of condensed milk in a pot of boiling water and boil for 3 hours topping up the water as you go.

Allow to cool then open tin and put caramel in a suitable container till ready to use.

For the tart tatin

Caramelize the butter and sugar in a suitable dish (8 to 10 cm).

Peel quarter and de-core the apple and place pieces on top of the caramel.

Roll out the puff pastry and cut a round disc just a little bigger than the size of the tatin dish. Place over the top of the apples and tuck the edges in. Bake in a hot oven at 180°C for approximately 10 minutes. Allow to stand for a few minutes before turning upside down.

To serve

Dress the plate with the caramel sauce, place the warm tart on it, add the ice cream and top with the caramel run out.

122
THE HORSESHOE INN

Eddleston, Peebles EH45 8QP

01721 730225
www.horseshoeinn.co.uk

Bardoulet's Restaurant in The Horseshoe Inn is the creation of husband and wife team, Patrick and Vivienne Bardoulet. When the property was acquired in 2005, it was extensively refurbished and before too long, the industry was taking notice of what was happening in the sleepy village of Eddleston, in the majestic Scottish Borders; 3 AA Rosettes and an EatScotland GOLD Award culminated in the award of AA Restaurant of the Year.

The classically elegant dining room has provided the perfect backdrop to Patrick Bardoulet's accomplished cooking as he brings the modern culinary techniques of his native France to bear on quality Scottish produce; Patrick balances classical flavours meticulously prepared with a contemporary flair to produce both stunning presentation and taste. The Horseshoe also operates a Bistro menu prepared by Patrick and his team for Guests who may prefer to dine in the Bar area. Whilst The Horseshoe Inn (invited members of Great Inns of Britain) was once the home of the village blacksmith, The Horseshoe Lodge was formerly the village Primary School; the 8 luxuriously individually furnished en-suite bedrooms (awarded 4 Stars by the AA and VisitScotland) are ideally suited for Guests who would like to explore Peeblesshire or visit Edinburgh on a short stay or for those wishing to stay-over after experiencing Patrick's A la Carte or Tasting Menu in Bardoulet's Restaurant.

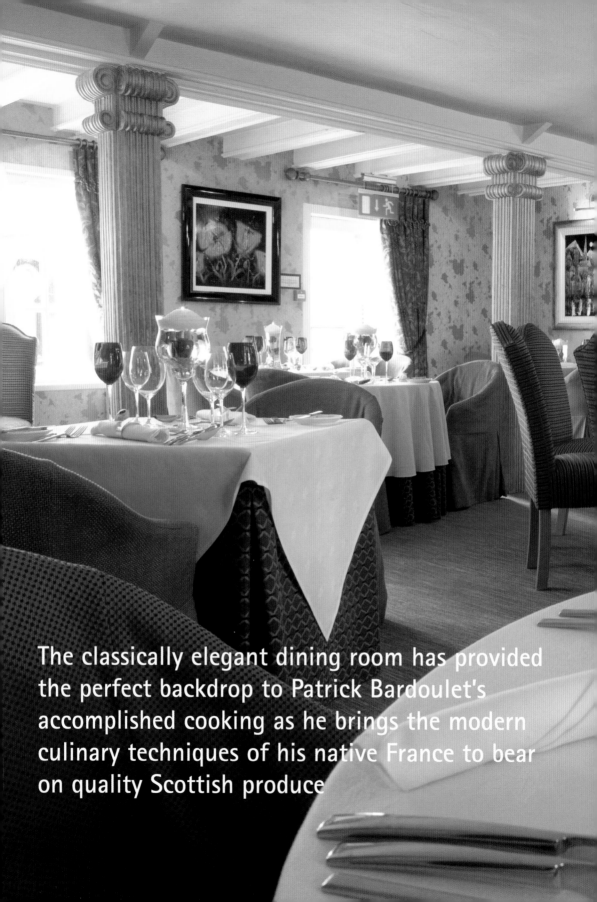

The classically elegant dining room has provided the perfect backdrop to Patrick Bardoulet's accomplished cooking as he brings the modern culinary techniques of his native France to bear on quality Scottish produce

ABERLOUR SALMON TARTAR WITH SPINACH MOUSSE, HAZELNUT SHORTBREAD AND LEMON MARMALADE

SERVES 2

Ingredients

280 gram of diced Aberlour salmon
1 diced shallot
salt & pepper
olive oil

Lemon marmalade

4 lemons
1.5 litre of water
250g of caster sugar

Hazelnut shortbread

80g of soft butter
20g of icing sugar
20g of egg white
120g of plain white flour
40g of ground hazelnut
5g of table salt

Spinach mousse

500g of spinach puree
1.2g of agar-agar

Method

Mix your diced salmon with the shallot, olive oil, salt and pepper.

Boil the water and sugar to make syrup wash and slice thinly the 4 lemons, remove the pips, put lemons on a tray covered with hot syrup at 150 ºC for 30 minutes.

Remove the tray from oven, cover with foil and allow to cool over-night.

Bring lemons and syrup back to boil, put it back in the oven at 150 ºC for 30 minutes. Then allow to cool.

Drain the syrup from the lemons, then chop the lemons and put aside in glass jar.

In a bowl mix the soft butter, icing sugar and egg white then add flour, salt and hazelnuts. Between two sheets of greaseproof paper, use a rolling pin and make to a thickness of 3 millimetres. Place in freezer for 20 minutes.

Pre-heat the oven at 160 ºC.

Remove the top sheet of greaseproof paper and with a sharp knife cut your shortbread mixture into 5 centimetre squares. Bake in the oven for 10 minutes.

Blanche enough spinach to make a 500 gram purée.

Heat the purée without boiling.

Add the agar-agar and whisk continuously for about 5 minutes.

Pour the mixture into a tray lined with cling film, put in the fridge and cut to shape when cold

To serve

Arrange as per picture.

SEARED FILLET OF WILD SEA BASS WITH SPICED TOMATO CONCASSE, CLAMS, ARTICHOKE AND HERB BUTTER

SERVES 6

Ingredients

Tomato & red pepper concasse

2 tablespoon of olive oil
pinch of 5 spices
4 tomatoes
1 red pepper

Garnish

2 large artichoke
80g of petit pois
1 carrot
10 centilitres of white wine
1 garlic clove
1 teaspoon of olive oil

Fish

800 gram of sea bass fillet
36 cockles
100 millilitres of white wine
10 centilitres of olive oil
knob of butter
salt and pepper

Herb butter

100g of soft butter
3 mint leaves
3 small sprigs of tarragon
3 sprigs of basil
5g of grated ginger
20 centilitres of fish stock
10 centilitres of whipping cream
¼ juice of lemon
salt and pepper

Method

Blanche the tomato, peel, cut, seed and dice.

Peel, seed and dice the red pepper.

Mix the diced tomato and pepper with spices together then cook in olive oil for approx 10 minutes until the vegetable water has evaporated.

Slice about ¾ inch to an inch off the tip of the artichoke.

Pull off any smaller leaves towards the base and on the stem.

Cut excess stem, leaving up to an inch on the artichoke.

Cut the artichoke into quarters and remove the cholk.

Put olive oil in pan and add the artichoke, add white wine and garlic and cook slowly for 5 – 6 minutes, set a-side.

In a pot of boiling water cook diced carrots until tender, boil fresh petit pois for 1 minute and refresh your vegetables under cold running water.

For herb butter

Boil fish stock and cream, add all other ingredients and blend.

For fish

Heat pan then add cockles and white wine and cover with lid for 1 minute.

In a non-stick pan heat olive oil then add sea bass on the skin side first, then add knob of butter to colour and season, cook for about 3 minutes then turn fish and cook on other side for less than 1 minute.

To serve

Drain artichoke, re-heat garnish with a little water and butter, blend herb butter to a foam and arrange on plate as per picture.

MORELLO CHERRIES WITH VANILLA SPONGE, PISTACHIO, KIRSCH FOAM AND CHERRY SORBET

SERVES 6

Ingredients

12 Morello cherries per person

Sorbet

500g of cherry purée
150g of water
150g caster sugar

Kirsch foam

260g of milk
40g of caster sugar
60g of kirsch

Pistachio

200g of pistachio
200g of caster sugar
200g of water
400g of pistachio paste

Vanilla sponge

Mix no.1

100g of egg whites
50g of double cream
50g of vanilla extract
5 split vanilla pods

Mix no.2

100g of plain white flour
200g of caster sugar
330g of ground almonds

Mix no.3 meringue

400g of egg whites
200g of caster sugar

Method

The previous day make your sorbet and vanilla sponge.

For the sorbet

Make syrup with your water and sugar and add cherry purée, freeze over night in your pacojet beaker or use an ice-cream maker.

For the vanilla sponge

Mix together mix no.1, sieve together mix no.2.

Mix no.1 and 2 together and add mix no.3

Pour the combined mixture into a cooking tin and cook for 20 minutes at 165°C.

When sponge is cooked remove from tray, cut into shape and store in an airtight container.

For the pistachio cream

Boil the sugar and water to make syrup and add the pistachio nuts and pistachio paste, blend until smooth and keep aside.

For the foam

Boil milk, sugar then add kirsch and whisk.

To serve

Arrange on plate as per picture.

132
MARTIN WISHART AT LOCH LOMOND

Cameron House, Dumbartonshire G83 3QZ

01389 722 504
www.martin-wishart.co.uk

The Internationally acclaimed Scottish chef Martin Wishart was invited in November 2008 by the directors of Cameron House Resort to open his second restaurant at the world renowned Cameron House Hotel on the bonnie banks of Loch Lomond. Cameron house is a wonderful retreat, a romantic and unforgettable escape with stunning loch views from this world class hotel.

Martin Wishart directs his team at Cameron House with his head chef Stewart Boyles and his restaurant manager Steven Strachan.

Head Chef Stewart Boyles began his culinary career at the age of 15 working for various private restaurants in Vancouver, Canada, where he was born.

Stewart is a naturally gifted chef with an exceptional understanding of how classical European kitchens operate. His training and knowledge he gained while working alongside Martin for over 4 years in Edinburgh shows in the professional way he runs his kitchen. The two chefs forged an excellent working relationship and Stewart took on the full responsibility of the new site with passion and commitment.

Most of the chefs employed to work under Stewart have spent extensive time working in Restaurant Martin Wishart in Edinburgh. This is the reason as to why the restaurant was awarded within 6 months of opening 3 rosettes by the AA Restaurant guide.

The menu is designed to offer the customer a large variety of seasonal ingredients. Many of these ingredients are sourced locally such as pike from Loch Lomond , langoustines and crab from the Isle of Skye and grouse, partridge and venison when in season from Ayrshire as well as Lamb and Beef from the borders. The wine list is an extensive and varied list of exceptional and affordable vintages from all over the world. Stored in the beautiful cellar which can be viewed from the restaurant.

Martin Wishart at Loch Lomond is every bit as luxurious as its sister restaurant in Leith, both restaurants share a similar ethos and style throughout. The restaurant's front of house staff are professionally directed by Steven Strachan a long standing senior manager from the Edinburgh restaurant and one of Scotland's most respected Maitre d'.

Steven clearly is a passionate and committed individual who can bring out the best from his restaurant team while delivering a relaxing and professional service for anyone dining at the restaurant. This is also reflected in Martin's vision for a memorable visit to Scotland's most beautiful loch and where guests can enjoy the spectacular beauty of Loch Lomond. The restaurant is located just 20 minutes from Glasgow international airport.

For more information visit our website:
www.martin-wishart.co.uk

Martin Wishart,
chef patron

Stuart Boyles,
Head chef

Jonathan Rivière

HALIBUT CEVICHE

SERVES 6

Ingredients

420g halibut
malden salt
15ml gastric
15g sugar
45ml lemon juice
5g salt
juice of half a lime
Tequila (to taste)
10g tomato fondue
1 tomato (skinned, de-seeded and diced)
1 sprig of fresh coriander
30g diced mango
10g passion fruit curd
coriander oil

Method

Dice the halibut into 1cm squares.

Season with Malden salt.

Whisk the lemon juice, gastric, sugar and salt together.

Add to the halibut along with the lime juice, tomato fondue and the tequila.

Finely chiffonnade the coriander leaves and add to the mix with the tomato dice.

To serve

Divide the mix equally between six 6-7cm stainless steel rings placed in suitable serving bowls.

Place the diced mango on top of the halibut.

Finish with the passion fruit curd and coriander oil.

*Photography for Martin Wishart
by Alan Donaldson*

ROAST WOODCOCK

SERVES 6

Method

Remove the giblets from the Woodcock and reserve for the paté.

For the paté

Heat a non-stick pan with 50g of the butter. Add the chicken livers and the woodcock giblets. Cook for 1-2 minutes on a high heat, then add a few thyme leaves and a tablespoon of the Armagnac. Season with salt and pepper. Transfer into a small blender and blitz until smooth. This paté is served with the woodcock on some toasted bread croutons.

For the woodcock

Cover the woodcock with the remaining butter and thyme. Season with salt & pepper. Warm a pan on the stove with a little oil. When hot, lay the woodcock in the pan and caramelise until golden on each side. Place the pan in the oven and roast the woodcock for 2-4 minutes, then remove and rest them for 10 minutes. Serve with some homemade bread sauce and the paté croutons.

For the bread sauce

Pour the milk into a pan. Add the onion and bay leaf and simmer for 5 minutes.

Stir in the breadcrumbs, add the butter and cream. Stir on a low heat for 5 minutes. Season with salt and fresh ground pepper.

Stir in the teaspoon of English mustard, remove the studded onion before serving the sauce.

Ingredients

pre-heat oven to 200°C, gas mark 6
6 whole woodcock
100g butter
2 sprigs of thyme
3 cloves of garlic
50ml Armagnac
100g chicken livers
salt & pepper

Bread Sauce

60g fresh bread crumbs
300ml milk
1 bay leaf
1 small onion studded with 3 cloves
30g unsalted butter
1 teaspoon English mustard
1 tablespoon of double cream
salt and fresh ground pepper

ECCLEFECHAN TART

SERVES 8

Ingredients

sweet pastry
70g unsalted butter
60g icing sugar
1g salt
1 whole eggs
200g plain flour

Filling

125g unsalted butter at room temperature
200g soft brown sugar
2 medium eggs
75g chopped walnuts
100g sultanas
75g raisins
75g golden raisins
zest of a lemon
zest of an orange
1 tbsp lemon juice

Method

For the pastry

Place the cold diced butter into a bowl with the flour, icing sugar and salt.

Rub together with your fingertips until it reaches a breadcrumb consistency.

Beat the eggs together and stir into the flour mix.

Knead the mix gently until it comes together into a ball.

Wrap in cling film and leave to rest in the fridge for at least 2 hours or overnight.

Butter and flour a 9 inch flan ring.

Roll out the sweet paste to 5mm thickness and place into the flan ring, pressing it into the corners. Prick the base with a fork.

Place back in the fridge for a further 30 minutes.

Line the tart with baking parchment or double layered cling film, and fill with baking beans.

Cook in the oven at 180°C for 20 minutes or until the pastry is cooked through.

Remove the beans, turn out the tartlet case and allow them to cool on a wire rack.

For the filling

Place the softened butter into a bowl with the sugar.

Using a hand blender, mix until light.

Incorporate the eggs to the mix one at a time.

Fold in all the dry ingredients along with the lemon juice.

Spoon the filling into the pre-baked pastry case and place back into the oven for a further 30 minutes, or until the filling is set in the centre.

To serve

Allow to cool and remove from the flan mould.

142
MICHAEL CAINES
AT ABODE GLASGOW

129 Bath Street, Glasgow G2 2SZ

0141 572 6011
www.michaelcaines.co.uk

ABode Glasgow launched in December 2005, following months of extensive refurbishment to the former Arthouse. Built in 1829 by Sir James Campbell, the historic Edwardian building was the family home of Sir Henry Campbell-Bannerman, who later became the first Glasgow-born Prime Minister from 1905 until 1908.

Located on Bath Street, in the city's cosmopolitan art district, ABode Glasgow is a growing group of stylish boutique hotels inspired by Andrew Brownsword and Two Michelin Starred Chef Michael Caines. Combining the charm of this listed building's many original features, such as the preservation of its white glazed bricks, Abode's vision is clear: to bring the best British values of tradition and quality, together with stunning contemporary style and personable service. As such, ABode Glasgow embodies something of the special character of Glasgow itself, which, from its hardworking Victorian heritage, has today emerged as one of the most vibrant and exciting destinations in Europe.

Since opening in 2005, Michael Caines Fine Dining at ABode Glasgow has consistently won many of Scotland's top restaurant and hospitality awards. Most

recently, these awards have included The Scottish Hotel Awards 2010 'Chef of the Year' for Executive Chef Craig Dunn and 'Restaurant Manager of the Year' for Alan Brady. Michael's belief that the finest cuisine comes from making use of local, regional and seasonal ingredients and produce has been interpreted masterfully by Glasgow born Executive Chef Craig Dunn. The Michael Caines Restaurant consistently serves imaginative and creative cuisine in an ambience in a relaxed, informal atmosphere.

Since opening in 2005, Michael Caines Fine Dining at ABode Glasgow has consistently won many of Scotland's top restaurant and hospitality awards

NEWHAVEN CRAB TART WITH BLOODY MARY SORBET

SERVES 1

Ingredients

Crab Mix

60g white crab meat
40g mayonnaise
25g brown crab meat
1g Cayenne pepper
½ lemon juice
1g salt
1g chives
3g roasted and peeled diced peppers

Bloody Mary Sorbet

1 shallot peeled & chopped
¼ cucumber peeled & deseeded
1 red pepper
2 tomatoes deseeded

Blitz the above and pass through a sieve

6 tomatoes deseeded
200ml of the above purée
2tbsp lemon juice
2tbsp tomato purée
2tbsp liquid glucose
few drops of Tabasco sauce
20ml vodka
salt to taste

Blitz the above and pass through sieve

Method

For the crab mix

Add the brown meat to the mayonnaise and mix in well, next add the diced peppers and cayenne pepper, add the white crab meat and mix well, finally add the lemon juice and salt and season to taste, reserve in the fridge until required.

For the pastry base

Roll out a 6"x 6" sheet of puff pastry to ½" thick brush with egg yolk and rest in the fridge for 30 minutes remove from the fridge and brush again with egg yolk. Place the pastry onto a heavy based oven tray lined with silicon paper place another sheet of paper on top and then another tray on top to stop it from rising. Cook in a pre heated oven 200ºC for 12 minutes. When ready brush with egg yolk this will give the tart a nice gloss finish. Use a 9cm pastry cutter to cut into discs.

To assemble the tart

Place the pastry in the centre of a round plate place a number 6 cutter on top and place the crab mix into the cutter. Pat down with the back of a spoon until smooth, spoon the bloody Mary sorbet on top of the crab, garnish with some micro herbs and confit tomatoes.

For the sorbet

Churn in ice cream/sorbet machine for 20 minutes until frozen.

Reserve until required.

LOIN OF BORDERS LAMB, CONFIT OF SHOULDER BOULANGERE, FENNEL PURÉE, LAMB TAPENADE

Ingredients

The Lamb, serves 1

120g lamb loin
40g spinach
2 confit garlic
25g sundried tomatoes
100g lamb shoulder
1 Red Rooster potato thinly sliced
25g lamb jus
10g olives

Confit of Lamb Shoulder, serves 4

500g lamb shoulder
750g duck fat
1 garlic clove peeled & sliced
3 sprigs of thyme broken by hand
20g course sea salt
5g whole black peppercorns crushed
5g whole white peppercorns crushed
20g ground cinnamon
2g five spice powder

Fennel Purée, serves 4

300g fennel
300ml water
75g unsalted butter
100ml chicken stock
1g cardamon
1g white peppercorns
1g fennel seeds
1g cumin seeds
3g salt

Lamb Sauce Tapenade, serves 6

1kg lamb carcasses chopped small
45ml olive oil
100g onions chopped small
100g leeks chopped small
100g carrots chopped small
1 head garlic cut in half
250g plum tomatoes
50g tomato purée
750ml chicken stock
250ml veal stock

Method

Mix together the salt, peppercorns, ground cinnamon and five spice. Scatter half on to a tray and then spread out half the garlic, thyme and bay leaf.

Place the boned shoulders of lamb on top and then sprinkle the remainder of the ingredient on top and cover with the cling film.

Leave in the fridge for 12 hours and then wash off under cold water and pat dry.

Place into a saucepan with duck fat and bring to the boil. Then confit at 100°C for approximately 1¾ hours very slowly cooking.

Once cooked and tender leave to cool Remove the shoulders from the fat and reserve until needed.

To assemble the boulangere

Cut the red rooster in half, Slice the red rooster on a mandoline 8 slices per portion, on a sheet of silicon paper lay 4 slices of potato leaving ½ inch gap between each slice. Give a gentle seasoning and place the lamb confit on top of the potato making sure all the potato is covered and there is a depth of around 1 inch of lamb. Repeat the same process with the potato placing it on top of the lamb. Spoon some of the lamb sauce over the potato place in an oven proof dish, cover with tin foil cook at 180°C for 25 minutes. When ready to serve, spoon a little more sauce over the potato.

For the purée

Make a small money bag with muslin cloth and tie up the spices.

Cut the fennel into thin slices and sweat them off in a medium thick based pan with the butter until soft and no colour. Add the chicken stock, water and spice bag and cook until the fennel is soft.

Drain the fennel into a sieve keeping the juice from the cooking liquor. Blend the fennel in a blender until smooth add some of the cooking liquor if the purée is too thick. Season with salt and pepper.

For the tapenade

Roast the lamb's carcasses lightly in the oven.

Separately, compote the onion, leeks, garlic, carrots in the olive oil, add thyme, cumin seeds, cinnamon and rosemary and sweat for a further 5 minutes.

Now add the tomatoes and tomato purée and cook out for 10 minutes.

Place the bones into a saucepan add the compote of vegetables, water, veal stock and chicken stock.

Bring to the boil, reduce to a simmer and cook out for 30 minutes. Pass through colander and then a chinoise and reduce to consistency required and finally pass through muslin.

COFFEE CARAMEL MOUSSE, CARAMEL ESPUMA, VANILLA BUTTER ICE CREAM

Ingredients

Toasted Almond Dacquoise, makes 1 tray at 20 x 20cm

5g plain T45 flour
30g ground almonds half toasted
30g icing sugar
1g salt
50g egg white
20g caster sugar

Caramel & Coffee Mousse, serves 4

50g caster sugar
20g water
100g cream
1g instant coffee
26g egg yolk
2.5g gelatine leaf
150g cream

Espuma Caramel, fills 300ml Espuma Gun

100g caster sugar
125g cream
125g milk
1.5 gelatine leafs

Caramel Semi-Liquid, makes 140 grams

50g caster sugar
30g glucose
60g cream
1g Maldon sea salt

Ice Cream Butter & Vanilla makes about 400ml

250g milk
50g caster sugar
50g cream
25g butter
6g milk powder
45g egg yolk
1 vanilla pod
10g caster sugar
1g stabilizer

Method

For the daquoise

Mix and sift flour, almonds, icing sugar and salt. Whip whites to meringue, gradually adding sugar. Sprinkle in the sifted flour and spread onto a tray. Sprinkle with icing sugar.

Bake at 180°C for 25 minutes.

Once baked cut 45mm rounds using a pastry cutter.

For the mousse

Boil the water and sugar to a dark caramel 165°C. Soak gelatine. Heat 100g cream and whip remaining cream to peaks. Deglaze the caramel with the hot cream. Pour a little over the yolks and then return to the pan and cook out to 85°C. Pass and cool to 60°C. Add the bloomed gelatine and coffee. Cool down further to 30°C and add a little whipped cream to emulsify. Pour over the remaining whipped cream and mix till smooth.

Use stainless steel 5 x 5 cm rings.

For the espuma

Soak gelatine. Make a caramel with sugar. Deglaze with cream and milk, bring to the boil. Whisk in bloomed gelatine. Pass.

Pour into an espuma gun and charge with 2 gases.

For the caramel semi-liquid

Cook the sugar and glucose to a dark blonde caramel. Deglaze with hot cream and add the salt. Cover and leave to cool.

For the ice cream

Combine the milk, milk powder and vanilla and refrigerate for 12 hours to infuse. Mix the stabilizer with 30g sugar. Heat milk infusion to 25°C and then add 50g sugar. Continue heating to 35°C and then stir in the cream and butter. Add the egg yolks at 40°C and then finally the stabilizer mixed with the sugar at 45°C. Continue cooking to 85°C. Pass and refrigerate for 24 hours to allow the mixture to mature. Churn using an ice cream machine.

To serve

Place a mousse onto the plate. Garnish with liquid caramel and quenelle of vanilla butter ice cream. Use either brandy snaps or a shot glass for the espuma.

152
THE PLUMED HORSE

50-54 Henderson Street, Leith, Edinburgh EH6 6DE

0131 554 5556
www.plumedhorse.co.uk

The Plumed Horse, established in 1998, relocated from Dumfries and Galloway and opened its Leith doors in December 2006. Continuing the general trend, it gains momentum day by day. Starting humbly, whilst showing promise, The (New) Plumed Horse's only awards were those garnered Tony Borthwick (2005 Scottish Chef of The Year) in its previous Michelin Starred incarnation. The first official glimmer of recognition for the "Edinburgh" venue came from the AA when they awarded 3 Rosettes to Tony and team in their second year of trading. Next was the return of the Michelin Star. This was augmented further by the AA Scottish Restaurant of The Year 2009-10 award. Now "Restaurant of The Year 2010-11" has been awarded by Catering in Scotland. All this was prior to its recent and impressive renovation. Full air conditioning, the bold, yet gentle, contemporary interior and friendly staff, fronted by Ian Bruce, all ensure a relaxed experience. Guests are invited to choose from a regularly changing, fairly short but substantial menu. Only the very finest produce is accepted by Mr. Borthwick. But that goes without saying! Also, The Plumed Horse takes pride in its extensive and reasonably priced wine list which boasts over 250 well chosen bins. You will be welcome at the Plumed Horse. It's a little like sitting in the proprietor's own private dining room. Book online www.plumedhorse.co.uk or by telephone.

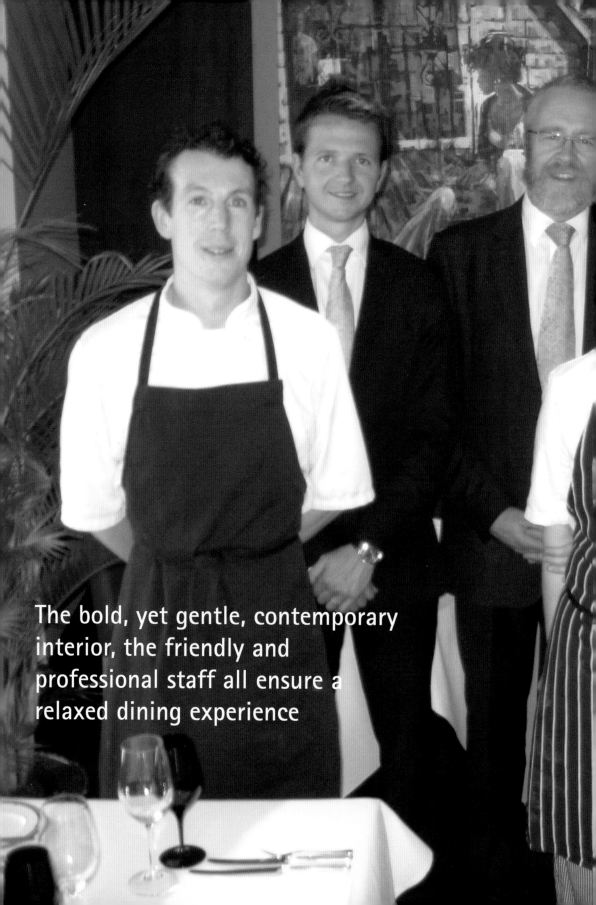

The bold, yet gentle, contemporary interior, the friendly and professional staff all ensure a relaxed dining experience

Head chef Tony Borthwick with his team

plumed HORSE

MILLE FEUILLE OF CRAB & LANGOUSTINES, PINEAPPLE, CHILLI & PASSION FRUIT

Method

Prepare the crab and make sure the meats are shell free. Store separately in the fridge.

Mix the brown meat with the butter and adjust the seasoning to taste. Add a little curry if you like. This needs to be soft textured.

Cook the puff pastry discs between two baking sheets to prevent it rising too much. Allow to cool fully and cut in half to make six thin discs. You only need three.

Make a chutney/salsa type dressing with the pineapple and the shallot (obviously, we make this in batches in the Plumed Horse), add some other flavourings if you like but keep it simple, some very finely diced green and red chilli, but be very careful with the heat!

Spoon a little of the pineapple dressing around the plate. Spread three discs thinly with the brown crab butter. Put a spot of mayonnaise in the centre of the plate and put a pastry disc on top.

Mix the white meat with a little of the mayonnaise that has been lightly flavoured with passion fruit. This should be done at the last minute as it will retain the freshness of the crab without it being tainted and overpowered by the mayonnaise. Put one third evenly on each pastry disc.

Sauté the langoustines in a little oil and clarified butter, leaving them a little under done, season with salt, fresh white pepper and lemon, cut in half along the length and put two halves on each disc.

To serve

Assemble the three pastry discs on top of each other, top with a little caviar and a sprig of chervil and serve immediately.

Ingredients

Ingredients per person

3 large langoustine tails, tracts removed, raw and shelled
35g white crab meat
20g brown crab meat
15g unsalted butter, soft
10g mayonnaise, homemade, flavoured with passion fruit
50g fresh pineapple, diced into 8mm cubes
20g very finely chopped shallots, a little very finely chopped chilli
3 x 6cm discs puff pastry

LOIN OF OLD SPOT PORK WITH PRUNES AND ARMAGNAC, CELERIAC, SHALLOTS AND GIROLLES

SERVES 10 - THIS DISH CANNOT PRACTICALLY BE PREPARED FOR ANY LESS

Ingredients

1/2 a whole loin of good quality pork, preferably Gloucester Old Spot

The front half (from the neck to the middle of the loin) is best for this dish

125g d'Argen prunes, soaked in Armagnac. The longer the better!

1 ltr diet coke

80g finely sliced shallots

2 large peeled cloves of garlic

5g fresh tarragon leaves

1 ltr strong chicken stock

100ml Harveys Bristol Cream

20ml sherry vinegar

80g caster sugar

500g peeled and sliced shallots

100ml Madeira

1 head celeriac

60 perfect Girolle, all the same size

1kg spinach

3 whole eggs

200ml whipping cream

Method

Start this the day before you need it.

Remove the meat in one piece from the bone and remove the skin. Cut out the eye of the loin and trim everything from it, retaining any good meat that can be used. Wrap tightly in cling film to keep its shape and refrigerate.

Trim a lot of the fat and all of the silvery sinew membrane from the inside of the fat. You need to leave the fat around 3mm thick. Trim the meat that is left on it to even it up.

Cut a pocket the whole length of the meat and put in the prunes, sliced shallots, tarragon and garlic.

Add all of the trimmed meat that is left, seasoning as you go. Roll it up and tie tightly with string.

Cook at 120°C in a fan oven for 20 minutes at a time, turning to lightly colour the fat. Keep turning it until it has some colour and then add the diet coke.

Keep on cooking until tender, probably 3 to 4 1/2 hours, depending on the pig itself.

When cooked, remove from the liquor and wrap in cling film immediately. Allow to cool. Refrigerate overnight. Store the remaining coke juices and fat in the fridge, allowing the fat to set on top.

The next day remove the stuffed part of the loin from the cling film and remove the strings, quickly wash off any fat that remains on the outside. Cut into nice even sized portions and wrap individually in cling film.

Remove the fat from the top of the liquor and warm the remaining juices, pass through a cloth.

Reduce the chicken stock by half and add the coke juices, bring to the boil and add 3/4 of the sherry, reduce to a saucing consistency.

Put a little water into a sauce pan and add the sugar. Make a golden caramel, add the sherry vinegar and allow to mix, add the remaining sherry and bring back to the boil. Remove from the heat and allow to cool. You now have your 2 sauces.

Cut the celeriac into 1cm dice and reserve. Trim the Girolles as necessary. Slowly roast the sliced shallots in the oven with a sprig of thyme until soft. Remove the thyme. Put the shallots into a pan with the Madeira, and boil the Madeira dry, purée the shallots and purée, season well.

Pick and wash the spinach, drain and put into a large pan. Cook only with the water that remains on the spinach after draining, when almost cooked, add the cream, bring to the boil and allow to reduce a little.

Purée in a liquidizer, add the eggs, season and pour into a flat tray to a depth of about 1cm. Cover in cling film without any air bubbles and cook in a low oven until set. Allow to cool then cut with a pastry cutter.

Cut the eye of the loin into individual portions.

Put the stuffed portions into a pan of hot water to heat gently for around 20 minutes.

Heat a black iron pan and seal the pork loin on all sides. Season with salt and fresh white pepper. They will only need a few minute in an oven so get the timing right.

Warm the sauce and use the caramel at room temperature.

Gently cook the celeriac in a pan with a little clarified butter until golden. Season and reserve.

Cook the girolles, season and reserve. Heat the shallot purée with a little whole butter.

Put the spinach disc onto the warm plate. It will heat up with the heat from the plate and the pork loin on top. Remove the hot stuffed loin from the cling film and put on top of the spinach. Arrange the celeriac and the Girolles on the plate, a dollop of shallot purée on too, place the remaining pork loin on top of the shallot purée and sauce with the 2 sauces. Serve immediately.

GATEAU

SERVES 5

Ingredients

400g dark bitter chocolate, over 60%
450ml whipping cream
110 Griottine cherries, with the
juices from the jar
50g glucose
1 large sheet chocolate sponge,
preferably flourless
chocolate shavings to garnish

Sorbet

500g cherry purée
30ml kirsch
150g glucose

Method

Churn the sorbet ingredients in an Ice Cream machine. Store in the freezer.

You need to work fast or the chocolate will start to stiffen.

Cut the chocolate sponge with a pastry cutter to give you 15 sponge discs. Sprinkle with a few drops of the cherry liquor. Drain the cherries well.

Melt the chocolate gently over hot (but not boiling) water, whip the cream to softly thicken and pour into the melted chocolate, mix well and add the glucose. Put it into a large piping bag to help fill the moulds.

Start with a ring mould off with a sponge, fill it with cherries, pipe in some chocolate and repeat until the mould is full, smooth off the top and allow to rest in the fridge for 3 hours.

To serve

Heat the outside of the ring mould with a blow torch gently and slide off the gateau. Allow to come round to room temperature and dress the top of the cake with cherries and chocolate shavings and serve with the cherry sorbet.

162
ROGANO

11 Exchange Place, Glasgow G1 3AN

0141 248 4055
www.roganoglasgow.com

Rogano has been a Glasgow dining institution since 1935. Its sleek Art Deco lines mirror the dining salons of the famous Clyde built Cunard Liner Queen Mary. Its style is synonymous when describing Rogano. From its famous frontage in Exchange Place to its bar and two restaurants, it encapsulates a trip in time aboard the great liners.

Inside the bar at Rogano it is an eclectic mix of local customers, always a warm welcome for travellers, the best of classic cocktails, prepared by experienced bartenders. The champagne and fresh Scottish oysters are worth the visit alone. The food keeps within this unique style. The menus lean towards seafood and shellfish coming from many local sources, game in season and aged beef feature on all market menus.

Café Rogano in the basement has a busy brassiere style with ever changing menus reflecting the Scottish seasons with lighter meals available.

The café is ideal for a stop whilst shopping in nearby Buchanan Street or for a pre-theatre dinner.

Rogano restaurant itself is a temple to fine Scottish seafood. The menu reflects Rogano's history with many classic recipes such as lobster thermidor, sole meuniere and fish and shellfish from Scottish waters adorn the menu as well as modern influences, prepared by Andy Cumming and his brigade.

The wine cellar holds many hidden gems and make Rogano a true Glasgow institution.

Chilled champagne in the bar, long leisurely lunches or light bites, afternoon teas, cocktails before and after dinner, rendezvous for drinks, wine and warm peaty malts in the evening

CRAB AND LANGOUSTINE WITH A PARMESAN WAFER, HERB SALAD

SERVES 4

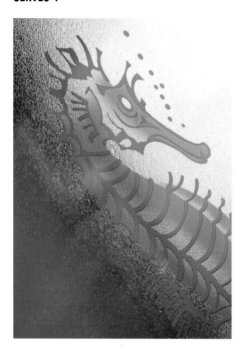

Method

For the parmesan wafers

Using a round scone cutter, sprinkle disks of grated parmesan cheese onto a non stick tray.

Place in a medium oven for 10-12 minutes until golden.

Remove from tray and allow to cool.

Makes approx 18 discs

Crab mix and langoustine

Mix the crab meat with mayonnaise in a bowl and add a pinch of cayenne pepper, salt and pepper and mix to a paste.

Peel the langoustine tails and remove vein.

Layer the parmesan wafers with a spoonful of crab mix and langoustine tail.

To serve

Garnish the top of the stack with picked fine herbs.

Ingredients

200g white crab meat
12 langoustine tails (cooked)
15g mayonnaise
250g parmesan cheese (grated)
30g selection of fine herbs to garnish
salt and pepper

PAN SEARED SEA TROUT WITH GOLDEN BEETROOT ROSTI, SCOTTISH GIROLLE MUSHROOMS, SAMPHIRE AND LEMON BUTTER SAUCE

SERVES 4

Ingredients

4 140g sea trout portions (approx 1 fish)
1 large golden beetroot (200g)
150g samphire
150g girolle mushrooms
1 lemon
50g unsalted butter
salt and pepper
50mls olive oil
1 egg yolk
10mls white wine vinegar

Method

For the rosti

Peel and grate golden beetroot, season with salt and pepper, place in a dish cloth squeeze all the moisture from the beetroot.

Put in a bowl and mix in 1 egg yolk.

In a round scone cutter, compact the beetroot firmly (repeat this 4 times).

Place rosti's on a cling filmed plate then put in freezer for 30-45 minutes to allow rosti to set.

Heat a frying pan with 25mls olive oil and fry rosti's (straight from freezer) for 2 minutes on each side or until golden brown.

Keep warm in oven.

For the sea trout

In a hot pan heat 5mls olive oil, place trout skin side down and season the fish.

Seal for 1 minute, turn the heat down by half and add a small amount of butter.

Cook for a further 2 minutes until skin is all golden colour.

Turn fish and cook for a further minute.

Take off the heat and allow to rest.

For the samphire and girolles

Rinse samphire thoroughly to remove any sand.

Clean girolle's with a fine brush to remove any dirt or small leaves. (Do not rinse)

Heat 5mls olive oil in a frying pan then sauté off the girolles for 1 minute.

Add 5g butter, a pinch of salt and pepper and juice of ¼ lemon to finish.

For the butter sauce

Reduce white wine vinegar by half then slowly whisk in butter until emulsified.

Add in juice of ¾ lemon.

To serve

Place rosti in middle of plate, sit sea trout on top, spread samphire and girolles evenly on a round plate.

Drizzle butter sauce around.

SCOTTISH STRAWBERRY PASTRY WITH CLOTTED CREAM ICE CREAM

SERVES 4

Ingredients

300g butter puff pastry (prepared)
500g Scottish strawberries
500ml double cream
50g caster sugar
½ vanilla pod, de-seeded
1 egg
Icing sugar to dust

Balsamic Caramel

40g soft brown sugar
40g unsalted butter
1 tablespoon balsamic vinegar
40ml double cream

Clotted Cream Ice Cream

300g clotted cream
150ml whole milk
5 egg yolks
115g caster sugar

Method

Roll out pre made butter puff pastry.

Cut into 15cm by 4cm strips.

Egg wash and dust lightly with icing sugar.

Bake at 225°C for approx 12 minutes.

Leave to cool.

Whip 500ml double cream; add caster sugar and vanilla seeds until firm.

Wash and prepare strawberries.

Slice puff pastry length ways and pipe one layer of cream on bottom, place strawberries on another layer of cream, then top with pastry and dust with icing sugar.

Repeat on top.

Dust with icing sugar

For the balsamic caramel

Place all ingredients, except cream, in a pan and bring to the boil.

Allow to simmer for 5 minutes then add cream.

For the clotted cream ice cream

Heat milk and cream in heavy based pan until boiling.

Remove from heat.

Whisk egg yolks and sugar until pale and golden in colour.

Pour over milk/cream mixture.

Return to stove and stir mixture continuously until it coats the back of a spoon.

Allow to cool.

Churn in ice cream machine until ready.

WEDGWOOD THE RESTAURANT

The Royal Mile, 267 Canongate, Edinburgh EH8 8BQ

0131 558 8737
www.wedgwoodtherestaurant.co.uk

Winner of Harden's Restaurant Guide, "Best UK Up and Coming Restaurant 2010" and a Fodor's Choice Award, Wedgwood the Restaurant is a key player in Edinburgh's restaurant scene. Creating the perfect night out in the perfect surroundings was Paul Wedgwood and Lisa Channon's basis for creating Wedgwood the Restaurant. The couple are deeply passionate about food and wine together with the whole dining experience. Surrounded by one of the best natural larders in the world, naturally most of the ingredients are locally sourced and the innovative dishes are all prepared by Paul in a creative international style.

Paul gains inspiration for his style of dishes from regular travels around the world. Favourite dishes in the restaurant include Panko and black sesame crusted Mullet or Tuna, chilli and coriander roulade with wasabi caviar as well as the recently introduced Salmon with biltong crust. Paul is also renowned for using interesting wild herbs and salads which are regular features on the menu. Many of these ingredients Paul forages himself.

With his vivacious and enthusiastic character Paul is often called upon to perform cooking demonstrations and he is a regular favourite at the Taste of Edinburgh Festival, as well as The Royal Highland Show.

Wedgwood the Restaurant also offers Wedgwood at Home, Wedgwood in the Office and Wedgwood in the Park. In short, if people aren't able to get to the restaurant or need to be elsewhere then Wedgwood the Restaurant can arrive in dinner party, canapé or picnic hamper format to almost wherever requested.

Surrounded by one of the best natural larders in the world, naturally most of the ingredients are locally sourced and the innovative dishes are all prepared by Paul in a creative international style

TOMATO TERRINE WITH VODKA & CHILLI JELLY AND CUCUMBER CONSOMMÉ

SERVES 6 - MAKES A SMALL LOAF TIN

Ingredients

12 large and very ripe tomatoes
½ tsp sugar
40 ml balsamic vinegar
salt and pepper

Vodka and Chilli Jelly

1 x 125ml bottle tomato juice
2 drops of Tabasco sauce
1 red chillies deseeded
2tbsp white wine vinegar
20 ml vodka
1¼ tsp agar- agar
pinch salt and pepper
150 ml vegetable oil placed in freezer for 30 minutes prior to commencing recipe

Cucumber Consommé

1½ cucumbers
4 mint leaves
2 basil leaves
2 tbsp fresh lime juice
couple of pinches of salt and pepper

Method

Score tomatoes and then blanch for a couple of seconds in boiling water, refresh in iced water, peel, quarter and deseed.

Lay on clean cloth to dry.

Season with salt and pepper and place in a bowl and pour over balsamic vinegar.

Leave for 1 hour and taste, adjust seasoning as required.

Line a small loaf tin with cling film leaving plenty overlapped to wrap.

Lay tomatoes flat in layers to fill mould and press down firmly and wrap over excess cling film, pierce the top of the film in a couple of places and place in fridge with a heavy weight on top. Chill to set for several hours.

For the jelly

Chop chillies very finely and place in a pan with all other ingredients except agar-agar and chilled oil and bring to the boil, simmer for 3 minutes. Strain.

Add agar-agar and dissolve slowly.

Fill a food injector syringe with the jelly mix.

Remove oil from freezer.

Slowly drip jelly mix into oil. This process will make the jelly set in small spheres.

Pour oil and jelly spheres into a sieve, drain off oil for future use and gently rinse off oil from jelly spheres left in sieve.

For the consommé

Put all ingredients into a liquidiser and blitz until smooth.

Strain through muslin and season to taste.

Refrigerate for use.

To serve

Cut 2 slices of terrine and place in bottom of a bowl, pour around cucumber consommé. Top with jelly spheres and place some spheres into consommé. Top terrine with a crisp basil leaf.

CONFIT PORK BELLY, WEST COAST DIVER CAUGHT SCALLOPS IN CAUL, CURRIED POTATO, CAULIFLOWER FRITTERS, SPINACH PURÉE

SERVES 4

Ingredients

Cure

180g salt
90g caster sugar

Pork

1kg slab pork belly
goose or duck fat to cover

Scallops

12 diver caught scallops in shell
100g Caul fat

Cauliflower Fritters

½ head cauliflower cut down into very
small florets
200g plain flour
40g cornflour
10g turmeric
15g black onion seeds
330ml good pale ale
pinch fresh yeast
flour for dusting

Curried Potato

500g mashed potato
100g unsalted butter
75ml double cream
10g curry powder

Spinach Purée

1 shallot finely chopped
300g spinach washed and stalks removed
25g unsalted butter
15ml veg stock
25ml double cream
salt and pepper

Method

For the pork

In a deep tray rub cure mix into the pork, cover with cling film, chill for 24 hours. Wash the pork off thoroughly and pat dry. Heat oven to 95°C, place fat into a deep tray just slightly larger than the piece of pork belly, it should have a lid or cover with foil. Heat gently. Once liquid put pork in on top ensuring it is covered by min. 2cm. Cover and cook for about 4 hours but check after about 3. When cooked press between 2 trays with a 2 kilo weight.

Refrigerate overnight. Cut into 4cm cubes, remove skin, leaving some fat intact. To reheat place fat side down in a warm pan and cook for 8 minutes 190°C.

For the scallops

Shell the scallops and pass through running water to clean. Place on cloth and dry for 2 hours. Wrap individually in cleansed caul fat, gently fry the scallops on all sides and baste.

For the fritters

Whisk all ingredients together to make smooth paste. Leave somewhere warm for 75 minutes.

Coat florets with flour and dip into batter mix and deep fry at 190°C for 90 seconds or until golden and cooked.

For the potato

Heat 50g of butter gently to melt. Add curry powder and gently fry for about 30 seconds. Pour in cream and add remaining butter and bring to boil, lower heat and slowly add mashed potato to the pan incorporating until you have a smooth but soft mash. It should very slowly slide off a spoon.

For the purée

Gently soften shallots in pan with butter. Add cream and stock and bring to boil. Leave to cool to room temperature. Add to food processor along with the spinach and blitz to a fine smooth paste.

To serve

On a long rectangular plate put 3 dessertspoons of potato purée at equal spaces apart on the left hand side of the plate and using the tip of spoon drag some purée across the plate. On the right side of the plate using a teaspoon make 4 pools of spinach purée again at even distances ending on the top right hand side of the plate and fill each gap with a scallop. Down the centre of the plate place the pork belly so each one sits on the potato purée. Scatter the fritters over the entire plate and drizzle with curry oil.

CAORUNN GIN, PINK PEPPER, RHUBARB AND VANILLA TRIFLE

SERVES 4

Ingredients

Cooking time 25 minutes
Prep time 45 minutes (plus cooling, infusing and chilling)

Rhubarb Jelly

4 rhubarb stalks peeled and peel reserved
3 pink peppercorns
250g caster sugar
100ml dry white wine
½ orange – zest and juice
25ml Grenadine
25ml Caorunn Gin
2 leaves gelatine softened in cold water

Pink Pepper and Vanilla Sponge

2 room temperature eggs
10 pink peppercorns crushed
40g caster sugar
1/2 vanilla pod seeds scraped
60g self raising flour finely sieved
10g melted unsalted butter

Custard

400ml double cream
½ vanilla pod split and scraped
8 egg yolks
75g caster sugar
3 juniper berries

Method

For the sponge

Preheat oven to 200°C. Whisk eggs, pink pepper, vanilla and sugar with an electric whisk for about 5 minutes until light, fluffy and doubled in volume. Sift in flour and carefully fold to incorporate fully, then do the same with the butter. Pour onto lined baking tray and bake for about 6 minutes until nicely golden brown. Leave to cool for 10 minutes then turn out onto a cooling wire and cool completely. Cut into shapes of trifle glasses and place in bottom.

Turn oven down to 170°C.

Cut rhubarb into 5cm pieces and then again into 3 strips lengthways. Reserve trimmings.

For the jelly and baked rhubarb

Put sugar, wine, rind, pink pepper, rhubarb trimmings and peelings, grenadine with 100ml of water and bring to the boil. Boil for 3 minutes and set aside to infuse. Place rhubarb strips into a roasting dish and strain syrup over rhubarb. Cover with baking paper then foil and cook for about 10 minutes until just tender. Leave to cool in syrup. Strain syrup again, add gin and drizzle a small amount over the sponge. Heat remaining syrup add gelatine (water squeezed out) and stir to dissolve. Set aside somewhere not too cool.

For the custard

Bring cream, juniper and vanilla to boil in thick bottomed pan. Set aside to cool. Whisk yolks and sugar in a bowl until light and fluffy. Pour in a small amount of the boiled cream mix onto the eggs to scorch. Add rest of cream mix very slowly a bit at a time, whisking all the time. Return mix to pan and with a thermometer on the back of a spoon keep stirring the mix over a low heat until the mix reaches 82°C. Remove from heat and quickly pour over sponge until glass is ¾ full. Gently tap the glass to even out the top and place on a tray and refrigerate.

When chilled pour over the rhubarb jelly until glass is nearly full. Finish with roasted rhubarb, rhubarb crisp.

182
RESTAURANTS IN CENTRAL SCOTLAND AND THE HIGHLANDS

WHERE TO LOCATE THEM

(1) AIRDS HOTEL, Port Appin, Argyll PA38 4DF

(2) THE ALBANNACH, Baddidarroch, Sutherland 1V27 4LP

(3) BLAIRS at the MERCURE ARDOE HOUSE HOTEL and SPA, South Deeside Road, Blairs, Aberdeen AB12 5YP

(4) KINLOCH HOUSE, Blairgowrie, Perthshire, PH10 6SG

(5) KINLOCH LODGE, Sleat, Isle Of Skye IV43 8QY

(6) LIME TREE, AN EALDHAIN, The Old Manse, Fort William, Invernesshire PH33 6RQ

(7) MALMAISON ABERDEEN, 49-53 Queens Road, Aberdeen AB15 4YP

(8) MONACHYLE MHOR, Balquhidder, Lochearnhead, Perthshire FK19 8PQ

(9) THE PEAT INN, Peat Inn, by St Andrews, Fife KY15 5LH

(10) THE TOLBOOTH, Old Pier, Harbour, Stonehaven, Aberdeenshire AB39 2JU

(11) TORAVAIG HOUSE HOTEL, Sleat, Isle Of Skye 1V44 8RE

(12) THE WATER'S EDGE at THE TOBERMORY HOTEL, Main Street, Tobemory, Isle Of Mull, Argyll PA75 6NT

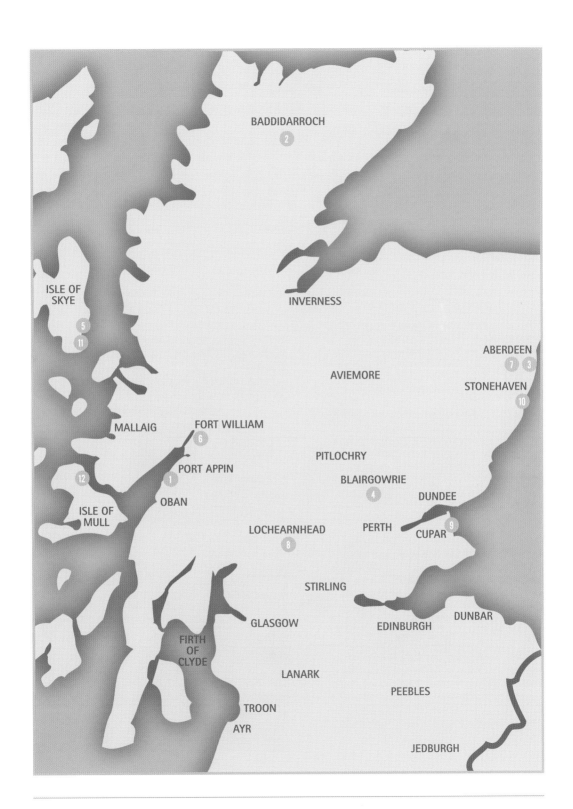

BADDIDARROCH
②

INVERNESS

ISLE OF
SKYE

⑤

⑪

ABERDEEN
⑦ ③

AVIEMORE

STONEHAVEN
⑩

MALLAIG

FORT WILLIAM
⑥

PITLOCHRY

PORT APPIN

BLAIRGOWRIE
④

DUNDEE

⑫

①

OBAN

ISLE OF
MULL

LOCHEARNHEAD
⑧

PERTH

CUPAR
⑨

STIRLING

GLASGOW

EDINBURGH

DUNBAR

FIRTH
OF
CLYDE

LANARK

PEEBLES

TROON

AYR

JEDBURGH

184
AIRDS HOTEL & RESTAURANT

Port Appin, Argyll PA38 4DF

01631 730 236
www.airds-hotel.com

The Airds has been privately owned and run for many years and is a member of Relais & Chateaux. Located on Loch Linnhe with the backdrop of the Morvern Mountains you could not want for a more stunning and peaceful hide away, with a welcoming ambience from the moment you arrive. With 11 individually decorated bedrooms and suites, many of them with wonderful loch and mountain views and a 2 bedroom self catering cottage set within the grounds, there is a choice for everyone.

Enjoy full afternoon tea in one of the stylish lounges where a roaring fire in winter will make you want to snuggle up with a good book or relax with an aperitif or indeed a night cap in the cosy bar, where there is an impressive display of Scottish whiskies, just waiting to be tried. The garden stretches down to the loch where you can enjoy a simple stroll along the shoreline, whilst for those feeling just a little more energetic, a game of croquet or putting is on hand before sampling the delights of our canapés prior to dinner.

The AA 3-rosette restaurant is reputed to be one of the finest in Scotland with fresh seasonal ingredients using local produce where only the finest quality will do. The Head Chef, Paul Burns, joined The Airds in 2001 and as a Chef there is no better place to live and work than in the Highlands of Scotland with some of the best seafood in the world right on the doorstep and Scottish beef and highland game not matched anywhere else.

Breathtaking landscapes, incredible views down towards the loch, this remote and peaceful setting epitomises classic west coast scenery, matched only by the quality of the service and cuisine of this 18th century converted ferry inn

LAMB FILLET SALAD WITH APRICOT PICKLED WOOD MUSHROOMS AND HERB LEAVES

SERVES 4

Ingredients

4 trimmed lamb fillets
200ml chicken stock
100g unsalted butter
2 fresh apricots (cut in half and de-seeded)
150g chanterelle mushrooms
75ml apricot brandy
25ml sherry vinegar
30g toasted pine nuts
selection of your favorite herbs
salt and pepper to season
olive oil for cooking
clove of garlic – peeled and thinly sliced
a few sprigs of thyme

Method

Warm apricot brandy, vinegar, 1 slice of garlic and thyme sprig. Add mushrooms and warm for a few minutes then leave to cook. This is done to infuse the flavours.

Heat oil and butter in frying pan and add apricots, cook both sides until tender. Remove apricots and keep warm. Add mushrooms and liquid to frying pan and heat until liquid has almost evaporated. Return apricots to the pan and keep warm. Rub lamb fillets with a little oil, garlic slices and thyme. Season with salt and pepper. Heat frying pan and flash fry lamb quickly turning as it starts to colour. Cook to your own requirements (pink is best). Remove lamb and keep warm. In the same frying pan add half the stock, reduce rapidly and add the remaining half. Reduce to a light syrup consistency.

Pass through a fine sieve and keep warm.

To serve

Carve the lamb fillets and place on the plate, add 1 apricot and place mushrooms on top of the apricot and lamb. Drop a few nuts over the top of the lamb and apricot and drizzle with meat juices. Arrange a few garnish herbs and leaves on the plate and enjoy.

WILD SALMON AND TURBOT BAKED IN PASTRY WITH MUSHROOM DUXELLE AND SEASONAL VEGETABLES

SERVES 4

Ingredients

4 x 80g skinned salmon fillet
4 x 80g skinned turbot fillet
1 egg beaten
80g chopped mushrooms
30g chopped onions
crushed clove of garlic
1 tbsp of chopped parsley
sesame seeds
splash of white wine
selection of pre-cooked vegetables of
your choice
puff pastry rolled flat and quite thin
(about 120-150mm – leave in fridge
until required)

Hollandaise Sauce

1tbsp fresh lemon juice
1 tsp white wine vinegar
160g butter
3 egg yolks
1tsp caster sugar
pinch of salt

Method

For the duxelle

Gently fry the onions and garlic in a little oil until tender. Add the mushrooms and fry gently until the moisture has evaporated. Splash with white wine until the liquid has again evaporated. Add a pinch of salt and pepper and add the parsley. Allow to cool.

For the pastry

On your work surface or on a dish, place the turbot, followed by a layer of duxelle and then place the salmon on top. Retrieve your pastry from the fridge and place the turbot/salmon/duxelle on top. Egg wash round the edges of the pastry. Fold the pastry by tucking in the sides, trying to keep the pastry tight at all times without breaking it. Turn over and place on a cooking tray so that the salmon piece is now at the bottom. Brush the pastry with egg and sprinkle on some sesame seeds. Cook in the oven until the pastry is golden, 180°C for approx 5 minutes. Leave to stand for a few minutes in a warm place.

For the hollandaise sauce

Place lemon juice and vinegar in a pan. Put butter in a separate pan. Place both on the hob and bring to the boil. Blend the egg yolks, sugar and salt in a liquidizer for 2 seconds. Add the lemon juice and vinegar slowly. Add the butter slowly with the liquidizer at top speed.

AIRDS' STRAWBERRY TART WITH COULIS

SERVES 4

Ingredients

4 x 8cm sweet pastry tarts (can be pre purchased in any good shop)
200ml double cream lightly whipped
50g icing sugar
1 vanilla pod (or vanilla essence)
200g strawberry jam (pushed through a fine sieve to remove seeds)
50g strawberries with stalks removed
few other berries of your choice to garnish

Method

Make the Chantilly cream by adding the double cream, sugar and vanilla pod together. (Split the pod in half and scrape out the seeds) Fold gently together and keep cold. Thinly slice 3 -4 strawberries for each portion and keep one unsliced strawberry for the centre of each tart to garnish.

Dip the garnish strawberries in the seedless jam to glaze them and put to one side.

Take each tart in turn and place a spoonful of cream in each and flatten down. Carefully arrange the sliced strawberries on top, over lapping until the tart is full. Place the glazed strawberry in the centre. Repeat for each tart.

Any remaining strawberries should be liquidized with a hand blender with the remaining jam glaze to make the coulis.

To serve

Place a drop of cream on each plate with the tart on top. Drizzle coulis on the plate and garnish with a few other berries of your choice.

This dish can be made either as individual tarts or as one large tart. Most Scottish berries can be used when in season as they all taste good.

194
THE ALBANNACH

Baddidarroch, Lochinver, Sutherland 1V27 4LP

01571 844 407
www.thealbannach.co.uk

O ver 21 years, chef proprietors Colin Craig and Lesley Crosfield have transformed the quirky; imposingly positioned 19th Century pile that is The Albannach.

Five rooms and suites, some traditional, some contemporary, share the house with the candle lit and intimate restaurant.

Everything looks to the sea and to the iconic dome of Suilven across Lochinver Bay. The way we cook owes much to the ocean's proximity.

For over two decades we have been respectfully handling the best that it provides, watching the boats land as we do so, but the hoof and the feather of Sutherland, Ross and Moray are not overlooked; nor are the Crofts of Assynt supplying herbs, fruits and vegetables, or Vineyards as yet to be found only much further afield.

Our efforts in the Kitchen have enjoyed much appreciated recognition of late, but along with others in this book, we regard the opinion of all those sitting in the restaurant as the prime concern.

Everything looks to the sea and to the iconic dome of Suilven across Lochinver Bay. The way we cook owes much to the ocean's proximity

MOUSSELINE OF WILD TURBOT, LOBSTER AND LANGOUSTINE, LOBSTER AND LANGOUSTINE SAUCE

SERVES 4

Ingredients

Mousseline

400g Turbot fillet
1 small, free range egg, beaten
125ml, double cream
pinch sea salt, pinch cayenne, tbsp chopped dill
pinch ground white pepper

Lobster and Langoustine

1 live lobster - 750g
8 large live langoustines
1 star anise (optional)
small onion, 1/2 celery stalk, small carrot, all
roughly chopped,
bay leaf
6 white peppercorns
tbsp parsley including stalks,
tbsp thyme
tbsp brandy
150ml dry white wine
1 large tomato
few drops olive oil
50g chilled unsalted butter
500 ml fish stock

Method

For the mousseline

Place Turbot and salt in processor or blender and whizz, add egg while running, blend until smooth, chill for at least 1½ hours.

Brush 4, 125ml Dariole moulds with melted butter.

Whisk chilled fish and gradually add double cream, whisk until quite stiff, pass through fine sieve or moulis, chill for 20 minutes.

Fold in dill, pepper and cayenne.

Spoon into moulds, 2/3 fill, tap bases to remove air bubbles, chill for 20 minutes.

Place in roasting tray, pour half filled with boiling water, cook in oven 180°C (gas 4) for 10 minutes until just springy to touch, remove from oven, rest in tray for a couple of minutes.

For the lobster and langoustines

Cook lobster in boiling salted water, with star anise for 12 minutes, cook langoustines in same pan for 5-7 minutes depending on size. Cool then remove from shells, reserve.

Divide the lobster meat into four attractive portions.

Sweat onion, celery, carrot with bay leaf and peppercorns for 5 minutes, add lobster and langoustine heads and shells and cook until hot, add brandy cook for 1 minute, add wine, cook for about 5 minutes then add fish stock, herbs and tomato, bring to boil then simmer for 25 to 30 minutes. Strain through a fine sieve then reduce by about half, add 75mls double cream, and reduce until it has thickened sufficiently to coat a spoon. Just before serving add a few drops of olive oil, heat until just simmering, then whisk in diced chilled butter. Keep warm.

To serve

Run a thin knife around the mousselines to release them from the moulds. Upend carefully onto plates and, if necessary, shake gently to release, arrange the langoustines and lobster around the mousseline then spoon some of the sauce around them.

ROAST SADDLE OF ROE DEER

SERVES 4

Ingredients

1 fillet of Roe deer saddle, trimmed of all sinew
and cut into 2 equal lengths, marinated in
3 dsp hazelnut oil overnight in the fridge
(About 100g of fillet per person)
300ml stock made from trimmings and
good meat stock
(The bones from the saddle, roasted with root
veg and then simmered for 2hrs is the best,
but beef stock added to the fried trimmings
is a good substitute)
100ml port
2 dsp brandy
180g unsalted butter cubed and chilled
1 whole cooked beetroot, sliced into 4 circles,
seasoned and lightly buttered
4 x 5cm pieces of peeled butternut squash,
pan-roasted and drizzled with white truffle oil
prepared broad beans if in season or fresh peas
3 large floury potatoes (Scottish Premier
or similar) boiled until just cooked with
skins on then skins removed
1 rasher streaky bacon
2 sprigs of thyme
2 tbsp goose or duck fat

Method

Take the meat out of the fridge 3 hours before serving time.

Set 4 x 7cm metal rings on baking tray, cover the bases with melted goose/duck fat, saving the remainder to moisten the potato mixture. Freeze this.

Fry the finely diced bacon until coloured. Add to chopped thyme, salt and pepper in a bowl with the skinned, crushed potatoes, reserving 4 potato slices for the frozen rings.

Line the rings with a potato slice and fill the rings with the potato mixture.

Press into the rings, cover with cling film and chill.

Reduce the port and brandy to a syrup, add the stock and gradually add the butter, whisking continuously until a glossy, coating consistency is achieved.

Put to one side.

To assemble

Cook the potato rings on their baking sheet on the stove top (preferably solid top) for about ½ hour, ensuring that they don't stick or burn.

When golden brown on the bottom, remove to oven 180°C (gas mk 4) for 10 minutes.

Roast the fillets on a pre-heated baking tray brushed with butter at gas mk 7 for 2 minutes less than the weight per piece in oz.

Rest for 5 -10 minutes.

Re-heat the root vegetables in the oven 180°C (gas mk 4).

Re-heat the beans briefly.

Re-heat the sauce, whisking, and adding boiling water as required to prevent splitting.

Place the beetroot centrally on the plate with carved slices of fillet on top.

Arrange the squash, beans and upturned potato galette around, and finally add the sauce.

DARK CHOCOLATE AND WALNUT PRALINE PARFAIT, PEARS POACHED IN RED WINE

SERVES 4

Ingredients

Pears

4 medium pears, peeled and cored
(leaving stalks)
¹/₂ bottle good medium red wine
250g caster sugar
400 ml water and a few drops of lemon juice

Custard

2 egg yolks.
¹/₂ vanilla pod split
50g caster sugar
150ml milk

Sponge Base

100g ground almonds
100g icing sugar
2 large free range eggs
3 egg whites
tbsp caster sugar

Parfait

Praline: 50g caster sugar, 50g walnut halves
100g dark chocolate at least 70% cocoa solids
150ml double cream
75g caster sugar
1 free range egg, plus one egg yolk
Glaze: made by melting 50g chocolate in
hot syrup made with 2tbsp water,
2 tbsp caster sugar and 1 tsp cocoa

Method

For the pears

Poach pears in syrup made by briefly boiling the water and sugar with the wine, gently simmer for about 1 hour (longer for firmer pears) or until pears are soft but not floppy.

Reduce some of the poaching syrup until thick sauce forms, then cool.

For the custard

Whisk eggs with sugar until light in colour.

Boil milk with vanilla scraping out seeds into milk.

Pour milk over eggs, whisking continuously. Return to pan and stir over low heat until thickened, pour through fine sieve into jug and cool.

For the sponge

Whisk egg whites until stiff then gradually add sugar until shiny.

Separately, whisk almonds, icing sugar and eggs until light and fluffy.

Fold together, spread on lined tray (400mm by 300mm) bake for 5 minutes at 220°C.

For the praline

Heat sugar slowly until mahogany in colour; add walnuts.

Cool on baking sheet, crush roughly with a rolling pin.

For the parfait

Heat sugar slowly with 2 tsp water until 120°C; whisk eggs and yolks, pour on the hot sugar, continuing to whisk until cool.

Melt chocolate; whip cream until soft peaks form.

Line the bases of four 50mm by 50mm mousse rings with sponge.

Fold elements together.

Fill the lined rings, smoothing the tops with a palette knife. Freeze for 2 hours.

To assemble and serve

Remove parfaits from freezer; spread some glaze on top, rest for 15 minutes.

Place pear upright on each plate, making some diagonal cuts in the lower half.

Using a blowtorch or gas lighter, heat the mousse rings to release parfait. Place next to pear, decorate with pear syrup and vanilla custard.

204
BLAIRS
AT THE MERCURE ARDOE
HOUSE HOTEL AND SPA

South Deeside Road, Blairs, Aberdeen AB12 5YP

01224 860 600
www.mercure.com

Set amongst beautiful surroundings and inspired by baronial buildings in the area such as Balmoral, lies Ardoe House Hotel & Spa. With 109 bedrooms, all traditionally decorated, Ardoe House Hotel caters for your every need. From relaxing bars, perfect for coffees or cocktails, to the full spa, offering an array of treatments. It is the perfect setting for a quiet break or an event.

It is also home to the award winning Blairs Restaurant. With a brigade of fantastic chefs, the team at Blairs are all dedicated and passionate about food and how they make it. Their concept is to spend lots of time and to go to great lengths to source the very best ingredients, from the finest suppliers, ensuring that all local produce is served at every dish. They like to treat the produce sympathetically by letting the ingredients speak for themselves and always try to enhance the natural flavours rather than detracting.

The success of the dishes comes from adhering to culinary logic and modernising the execution, sometimes introducing some unexpected twists with the main emphasis always being the combination of flavours. This has resulted in Blairs Restaurant being awarded its first Rosette for its outstanding food quality and service.

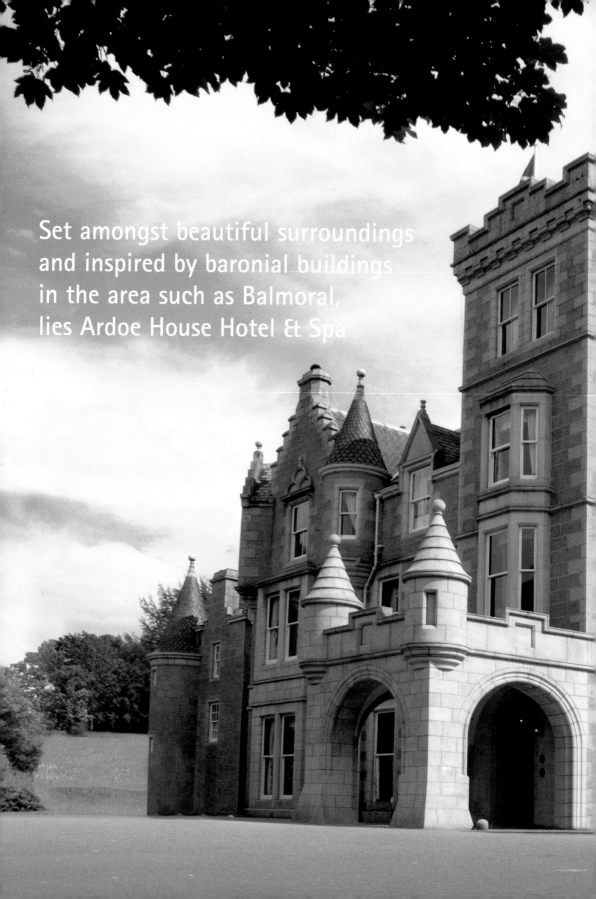

Set amongst beautiful surroundings and inspired by baronial buildings in the area such as Balmoral, lies Ardoe House Hotel & Spa

PAN FRIED RED MULLET, CAPPUCCINO OF SHETLAND LANGOUSTINES, SAFFRON VERMICELLI, LANGOUSTINE OIL

SERVES 4

Ingredients

8 fresh Red Mullet fillets
25ml brandy
8 live langoustine
250ml double cream
500g Vermicelli noodle
100g tomato purée
1ltr fish stock
micro shoots
2g saffron
50g lecithin
1 med onion
250ml whole milk
2 carrots
1 fennel

Method

Make strong fish stock adding saffron at the end. When cold soak the Vermicelli over night, and store in the stock for service. Pin bone and neatly square off and score the mullet, rub the skin with saffron oil, set aside until ready to serve. Peel and skewer langoustines for service (2 per portion). Roast the langoustine shells and heads in the oven with chopped carrot, onion, leek, garlic and tomato purée. Add to a large pan and flambé with brandy, add some chopped tomato and cream, bring to the boil and simmer, liquidise all together and pass. Separate bisque into 2 pans. Reserving 1 as is and add the whole milk and lecithin to the other and warm.

To serve

Pan fry the Mullet Skin side down. Warm the bisque in a pan and gently poach the langoustines. In a serving bowl spoon a small pool of the Shellfish Bisque, arrange the mullet in a criss-cross in the bowl with the langoustines arranged on top. In a pan with boiling salted water warm the Vermicelli and quickly give a toss in the langoustine oil using a fork, arrange on top of the mullet. Using a stick blender blitz the bisque and lecithin mix to form a foam, and drape over the dish. Finish with dressed and seasoned shoots (if shoots are not available then add a sprig of chervil).

FILLET OF VEAL, BRAISED OSSO BUCCO, PARSLEY CREAM, GIROLLE MUSHROOMS, PAN JUICES

SERVES 4

Ingredients

1 whole veal fillet

2 ltr veal or good quality beef stock

5kg shin of veal

1kg pigs caul

2 carrots roughly chopped

600g Girolles

2 onions

1ltr double cream

2 sticks celery roughly chopped

4 large potatoes

1 bunch thyme

I bunch sage

2 yellow courgette

2 green courgettes

Method

Roughly chop all vegetables. Heat a large frying pan, and seal the shin of veal, ensuring it is well caramelised. Place in a casserole dish, and using the frying pan fry off the vegetables and also add to the casserole. Add a sprig of sage and garlic, cover with a lid and cook in the oven for 4 hours at 120°C. Strain liquid and reduce on the stove, reserving around half for the finished dish.

In the mean time shred the meat and place in a bowl. Roll out cling film. Add reduced liquid to the meat, this will act as both seasoning and a binding agent for the meat. Place on the cling film to form a sausage shape using the cling film to roll it tight. Try and get this roll about the same diameter as the veal fillet for presentation. Place this roll in the fridge to set. Once set cut into portions about 5cm high and wrap in the pigs caul, this will help it keep its shape. Set in the fridge.

Using a hot pan sear off all sides of the seasoned veal fillet, finish with sprinkling of garlic and sage and remove from pan, allowing to cool slightly. Once cooled repeat rolling process with the cling film and portion, roughly the same size as the shin, set aside with the cling film still on. Leave on to cook.

For the garnish

Top and tail the potatoes and cut into a cylinder using a tall fondant cutter, place in a deep tray with beef stock, and add a slice of butter on top of each. Bake in the oven at 180°C until potatoes have absorbed most of the liquid and are golden. Slice the courgettes length ways using a mandolin. Blanch these in boiling salted water and refresh in iced water. Lay out on cloth. Take a green slice and lay flat, seasoning with a leaf of sage and roll, repeat process, alternating the colours until it gets to about the same size as the other elements. Place in a dish with a little white wine, and cover with tin foil and heat through the oven.

For the parsley cream

Sweat a little onion with some garlic, add a little white wine and reduce, add cream and reduce again. Blanch and refresh a good bunch of flat leaf parsley and spinach, liquidise with the reduced cream, pass and adjust seasoning.

To serve

Place the veal fillet and shin in the oven at 195°C with a small knob of butter and seasoning for 12 minutes (medium/rare). Allow to rest, meanwhile using a rubber paint brush give a long stroke of parsley cream along the centre of a long plate and place the fondant potato at one end and the courgette roll at the other. Once the meat has rested, remove the cling film and using a knife cut off one end to expose the pink flesh. Arrange along the cream strip, with a nice line of sautéed girolles and finish with the veal jus.

HOT CHOCOLATE FONDANT ORANGE AND MINT PARFAIT

SERVES 4

Ingredients

Hot Choc Fondant

675g dark chocolate
500g whole egg
450g butter
300g egg yolk
300g sugar
250g flour

Orange & Mint Parfait

1 lt fresh orange juice
200g sugar
250g fresh mint leaves
1lt cream
orange zest (6 oranges)
350g egg white

Method

For the fondant

Melt chocolate in a double boiler and add the butter. Whisk the egg yolks and egg until fluffy. Add the sugar and whisk mix in the melted chocolate, and fold in the flour. Pipe into greased dariole moulds, only fill around ¾ of the way up, and freeze. Cook from frozen at 180°C for 6 minutes.

For the parfait

Whip cream and set aside. Reduce orange juice. Boil the sugar with a little water, whip egg whites and pour in the syrup and whisk until a soft peak, Italian meringue is achieved. Fold in the whipped cream and fold in the orange reduction, the zest and the mint purée. Pour into mini timbales and freeze.

KINLOCH HOUSE

Blairgowrie, Perthshire PH10 6SG

01250 884 237
www.kinlochhouse.com

Kinloch House, owned and run by the Allen family, stands on a gently sloping hillside looking out over a wide lush valley, the heartland of some of Scotland's richest agricultural acres and the centre of the soft fruit growing industry.

The house was built in1840, when it was fashionable for the newly rich industrialists from the jute trade, to establish seats for themselves in the country, and Perthshire, with its salmon rich rivers and grouse moors provided the perfect environment. Kinloch House is a fine example of a Scottish country house with log fires, oak panelled hall and first floor portrait gallery, and stands in 25 acres of wooded policies and parkland.

There are eighteen bedrooms including three suites and four ground floor rooms all with modern facilities. There is also a 35 foot long pool with sauna, steam room and spa bath and a treatment room offering a list of beauty therapy treatments.

Head chef, Steve MacCallum, assisted by his talented team Steve Rae and Robbie Mattinson, make full use of an abundance of ingredients for which the area is famous, such as a wide variety of game, Aberdeen Angus beef, fish, shellfish and soft fruits. Steve ensures that there is a consistency of performance in the kitchen and a belief in the value of freshness and quality. Kinloch House is an ideal venue to unwind and relax from the pressure and stress of modern life.

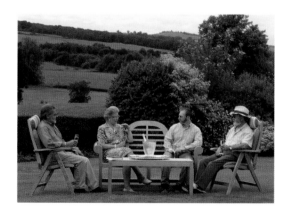

Kinloch House is a fine example
of a Scottish country house with
log fires, oak panelled hall and
first floor portrait gallery

ROAST BREAST OF WOOD PIGEON WITH GREEN BEANS, GLOBE ARTICHOKE, CHANTERELLES AND A DEEP FRIED EGG

SERVES 4

Ingredients

2 wood pigeons
200g chanterelles
50g butter
200g cooked green beans
100g shallots
2 globe artichoke
1 clove garlic
4 hens eggs
1 sprig of thyme
½ litre brown chicken stock
200ml madeira
flour
2 beaten eggs
breadcrumbs

Method

Remove legs and wish bone from pigeons then sauté pigeons in 25g of butter till golden brown then place the pigeons on a tray and roast in a hot oven for 8 minutes. Remove and rest.

Put the legs in a pan and add sliced shallots and chopped garlic and sauté until brown.

Add madeira, reduce till syrupy and add thyme and chicken stock and reduce slowly by half and pass through sieve into clean pan, taste and season.

Gently sauté sliced, trimmed artichoke hearts in a little butter until tender.

Gently sauté chanterelles in a little butter.

Poach the egg till the white is set and yolk still soft, remove and chill in iced water.

Trim eggs to an even round shape, using a cutter, then coat in flour, beaten egg and breadcrumbs.

To serve

Warm pigeon sauce, add chanterelles, artichoke and green beans and season. Remove pigeon breasts from carcasses, and slice thinly.

Deep fry eggs at 180°C for 1 minute till golden.

Place some green beans, artichoke and chanterelles on warm plates.

Thinly slice pigeon breast and place on top, pour over sauce and top with the deep fried hens egg.

FILLET OF WILD SEA BASS WITH BROWN SHRIMPS, PEA PURÉE, SAMPHIRE AND A CHIVE AND LEMON BUTTER SAUCE

SERVES 4

Method

Cook peas in chicken stock for two minutes, drain, liquidise and pass through a sieve, set to one side and keep warm.

Place chopped shallots, vinegar and white wine into a pan and reduce till syrupy.

Whisk in butter till smooth.

Add lemon juice and a pinch of salt, strain through a sieve, cover and keep warm.

Lightly season sea bass fillets and pan fry in a little oil for two minutes, remove and set aside in a warm place.

Cook spinach in a little butter and place in the centre of a plate.

To serve

Spoon pea purée around.

Place the sea bass on top of the spinach.

Place chives, peas, broad beans, tomato, samphire and shrimps in the butter sauce, gently warm through and spoon around the sea bass.

Ingredients

4 x 150g portions of sea bass
2 finely chopped shallots
1 tbsp white wine vinegar
200ml dry white wine
250g unsalted butter
pinch of salt
juice of half a lemon
200g peas
500ml chicken stock
200g cooked samphire
2 tomatoes, peeled and the flesh diced
200g spinach
200g cooked peas and broad beans
200g brown shrimps
2 tbsp chopped chives

ELDERFLOWER AND SUMMER BERRY JELLY WITH CREAM AND SHORTBREAD BISCUITS

SERVES 4

Ingredients

Jelly

10 elderflower sprays
strawberries
250g sugar
raspberries
250ml water
brambles
juice of 2 lemons
blackcurrants
5 leaves gelatine
500ml double cream

shortbread

600g plain flour
300g butter
150g caster sugar

Method

For the jelly

Warm the elderflowers, sugar, water and lemon juice for 5 minutes and add softened gelatine leaves and stir gently until the gelatine has dissolved. Strain the liquid into a jug.

Fill small moulds with mixed berries and top up with jelly. Place in fridge to set.

For the shortbread

Preheat oven to 150°C.

Cream the butter and sugar until smooth then gently mix in the sieved flour. Wrap in clingwrap and rest in the fridge for 30 minutes.

Roll out dough to a thickness of 5mm and use a cutter to make rounds.

Place on a lightly buttered tray and bake for about 30 minutes. Remove from tray and place on a wire rack, sprinkle with caster sugar and leave to cool.

To serve

Whip cream.

Dip jelly moulds into hot water to loosen.

Turn onto plates, serve with strawberries, shortbread and a spoonful of whipped cream.

224
KINLOCH LODGE

Sleat, Isle of Skye IV43 8QY

01471 833 333
www.kinloch-lodge.co.uk

Kinloch Lodge is set in the unrivalled beauty of the Isle of Skye which was recently named the "Fourth Best Island in the World" by National Geographic. Situated amongst the mountains of Skye and the fresh sea waters, Kinloch Lodge is the ultimate romantic escape for the gastronome. The family run 3 AA rosette restaurant which holds the Scottish islands' only Michelin Star was started by award-winning cookery writer Claire Macdonald in 1973. Local seafood, venison and game are cooked to perfection in innovative ways by head chef Marcello Tully who never tires in his enthusiasm for one of the best larders in the world situated on his doorstep. The extensive wine list takes guests on a fascinating international journey whilst the whisky collection takes guests from the highlands and islands to the lowlands of Scotland. Kinloch is also well known for its Wine Flights which is a tasting menu with two wines matching each course. The luxuriously appointed 15 double bedrooms each have spectacular views of the dramatic, surrounding landscape and the three drawing rooms have roaring log fires and deep sofas.

Awarded the Romantic Hotel of the Year at the Scottish Hotel Awards 2010, Kinloch Lodge is a perfect haven to escape to for a dose of rest and relaxation at any time of the year.

Both Claire Macdonald and Marcello Tully run a number of cookery courses and demonstrations at Kinloch Lodge throughout the year for those looking for something a bit different.

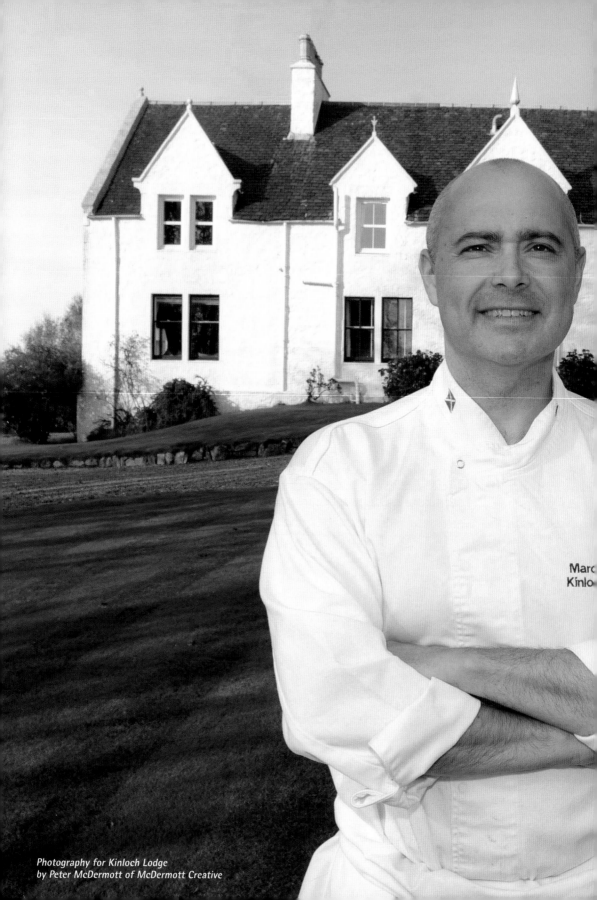

Marc
Kinlo

*Photography for Kinloch Lodge
by Peter McDermott of McDermott Creative*

Local seafood, venison and game are cooked to perfection in innovative ways by head chef Marcello Tully who never tires in his enthusiasm for one of the best larders in the world situated on his doorstep

FILLET OF HAKE, WITH MUSSELS AND PARSLEY CREAM SAUCE

SERVES 6

Ingredients

1 fairly large aubergine
12 asparagus spears
2 red peppers
olive oil
1 litre best quality fish stock
500ml double cream
2 handfuls parsley, chopped finely
360g uncooked mussels – washed and scrubbed
6 hake fillets, each weighing about 120-130g
100ml water

Method

Put the mussels in a pan and add 100ml water. Simmer for 1 minute with the lid on the pan, or until the mussels have opened. Be sure to throw out any mussels which remain closed once cooked; this indicates that the mussels were dead before being cooked, and the danger is that there is no way of knowing how long they had been dead.

Slice both ends off the aubergine and each red pepper. Slice both lengthways, in slices no thinner than ½ cm. Remove the woody part of the asparagus stalk and brush each slice and spear both sides with olive oil. Chargrill on a high heat for approx 45 seconds each side. Remove and keep warm.

Reduce the fish stock by about half by boiling it. Add the double cream and continue to simmer for 5 mins. Season this with salt and pepper. Stir in the parsley just before serving.

Sear the hake fillets in a hot pan with a knob of butter, about 3 mins each side, cooking skin side first.

To serve

Put a slice of the chargrilled pepper and aubergine onto each plate. Put a hake fillet on top of the vegetables, with the skin facing upwards, and 2 asparagus spears on top of this. Put the mussels around the fish and vegetables and generously spoon the fish sauce over everything.

MARCELLO TULLY'S PORK CHEEKS WITH MONKFISH WRAPPED IN PARMA HAM, WITH PASSION FRUIT SAUCE

SERVES 6

Ingredients

6 pork cheeks
360g monkfish fillet
8 slices Parma ham
1 carrot
½ leek
1 parsnip
salt and pepper

Passion Fruit Sauce

2 passion fruit
40ml whisky
50ml Canadian maple syrup
1 star anise
20ml beef jus

Beef Jus

800ml beef stock
150ml red wine
160g redcurrant jelly
salt and pepper

Method

Lay out the Parma ham slightly overlapping to form a layer. Place a whole monkfish fillet, which has been seasoned with salt and pepper in the centre. Roll and wrap tightly with cling film. Cut into 6 pieces once chilled.

Brown the pork cheeks in very hot oil on both sides and season with salt and pepper.

Put the pork cheeks in a casserole dish and add the roughly chopped vegetables, cover with water.

Cook for 6 hours, with a lid, at 130°C, making sure the pork cheeks are always covered with water.

Steam the monkfish for 8 minutes.

For the sauce

Remove seeds and pulp from passion fruit and place in a small saucepan.

Add star anise and whisky, heat then flambé.

Then add maple syrup and beef jus and simmer for 5 minutes.

For the beef jus

Add these ingredients to a pan and reduce, then pass through a sieve.

To assemble

Place a piece of monkfish in Parma ham on each plate, place a pork cheek next to it and drizzle over the passion fruit sauce. Garnish with a piece of crispy Parma ham (optional).

MARCELLO TULLY'S CHOCOLATE AND ORANGE DESSERT

SERVES 6

Ingredients

200ml water
2 teabags
125g butter
75g soft brown sugar
150g breadcrumbs
1 tsp vanilla essence
12 eggs
50ml Baileys
445g caster sugar
730ml double cream
5 oranges juice
1 orange zest
50ml Cointreau

Chocolate Topping

150g dark chocolate
30g double cream
30g butter

Method

Boil water and pour over the tea bags, remove tea bags once water has infused.

Melt butter and add brown sugar and 20g caster sugar, heat to make a caramel.

Stir in breadcrumbs, vanilla essence, 3 eggs, 50g of the caster sugar, 230ml cream, tea and Baileys to the caramel. Beat well.

Cream the remaining caster sugar and eggs together, add all the remaining ingredients to form the orange layer.

For the chocolate topping

Gently melt the ingredients together.

Then compile: tea mix 35g, orange mix 45g and chocolate mix 12g into a ring.

Chill to set.

To serve

Drizzle some of the chocolate mixture onto each plate, remove the dessert from the ring and place on top.

234
LIME TREE
AN EALDHAIN

The Old Manse, Fort William, Invernesshire PH33 6RQ

0139 770 1806
www.limetreefortwilliam.co.uk

At the west end of Fort William High Street overlooking Loch Linnhe and the mountains beyond is the Lime Tree An Ealdhain – a former 1850 Church Manse which has been lovingly refurbished and expanded to create a stylish hotel, award winning restaurant and high quality art gallery capable of hosting exhibitions from touring national art collections. The business gets its name from the ancient Lime Tree in the garden. An Ealdhain is Gaelic, meaning 'the creative place'.

Visit the Lime Tree An Ealdhain and take the opportunity to relax in our Victorian lounges with their open fires or to research your next day on the hills in our Map Room. Our restaurant is open plan so you will see, hear and importantly be able to enjoy the aroma of your meal being prepared for you.

The ethos of the Lime Tree An Ealdhain is that our food should be made from fresh, seasonal ingredients sourced locally where possible. Head Chef Ross Sutherland then creates menus to combine the creativity and skill of the chef team with the best of ingredients. Together with comfortable, stylish ad individual accommodation, The Lime Tree is a place to relax - to feel at home in the heart of the Highlands.

Lime Tree An Ealdhain gets its name from the 200 year old Lime Tree found in the garden and An Ealdhain is Gaelic and means 'the creative place'

SMOKED DUCK BREAST, TRUFFLED GOAT'S CHEESE PANNA COTTA AND MAPLE SAUCE

SERVES 4

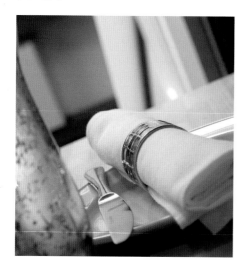

Ingredients

Panna Cotta

300ml cream
200ml milk
150g goat's cheese
1 ½ gelatine leaf
truffle oil
10g fresh truffle

For the maple sauce

75ml maple syrup left from coating
the duck breast
50ml chicken stock
50ml game stock

For the smoked duck

4 duck breasts
75ml maple syrup
salt and pepper
smokery wood chips

Method

For the panna cotta

Put 300ml cream and 200ml milk in a pot on low heat. Put the gelatine leaf in cold water until soft. Put goat's cheese in a food processor until smooth, then grate fresh truffle as fine as possible before adding to goat's cheese. Now add the hot milk and cream mixture to the food processor, and, while mixing, add truffle oil to taste. Squeeze out the water from the gelatine and add it to the hot panna cotta mix then pass through sieve into moulds. Place moulds in the fridge for four hours or until set.

To make the smoked duck

Trim the excess fat from the back and side of the beast, then score the fat. Add the duck breast, fat side down to a cold pan, put on a low heat. Season the back of the breast with salt and pepper. The fat will render out of the duck; keep taking the fat out of the pan. Keep cooking until the fat is thin and crispy and then turn over the duck and cook for 2 minutes on the back. Add the maple syrup and raise to a high heat while constantly spooning the mix over the duck. Now take the duck out and put it on a smoking rack. Put your wood chips in a tray, smoking without flames. Smoke duck over the top with a lid for three minutes then remove and cool.

For the sauce

Use the maple syrup left in the pan from cooking the duck, add the chicken stock and game stock to maple syrup and reduce until thick, then pass through a sieve and leave to cool.

To serve

Slice the duck, un-mould the panna cotta by dipping the mould in hot water for a few seconds, then arrange both on plate and finish with the sauce.

SCOTTISH RABBIT AND LANGOUSTINE BALLOTINE WITH BABY VEG AND BRAISED LITTLE GEM LETTUCE

SERVES 4

Ingredients

Rabbit Ballotine and Best End

best end of rabbit
langoustines
Parma ham
salt and freshly ground black pepper

Carrot Purée

50g shallots, peeled, finely chopped
10g unsalted butter
200g carrots, peeled, finely chopped
chicken stock
salt, to taste
sugar, to taste

Pea Purée

200g frozen peas
salt, to taste

Light Game Jus

rabbit bones
chicken stock
onions
carrots

Garnish

baby carrots
baby leeks
broad beans, out of their pods, inner
membrane removed
micro pea shoots
little gem lettuce

Method

Shell all raw langoustines.

To make the Ballotine put 2 sheets of Parma ham on cling film, put the rabbit loins side by side then put raw langoustines in the middle, season with salt and pepper roll Parma ham over then fold over cling film to make a sausage, twist ends.

Trim up best end, clean up bones (French trim style), tinfoil over bones so that you don't get burned while cooking.

Soften sliced onions and carrots in oil then top up with chicken stock, turn heat up to boil. Cook carrots, boil until soft then blend in food processor. Add butter while blending, season to taste, pass through a sieve.

Brown off rabbit bones in oven then add to a pot with vegetables. Cover with chicken stock, cook for 30 minutes then pass and reduce to right consistency, then season.

Put water on to boil, add frozen peas and cook for 2 minutes, then blend in food processor. Add seasoning to taste, pass through a sieve.

Put rabbit Ballotine in water, bath at 62°C for approx 20 minutes then pan fry to crisp up Parma hams. Add racks to pan baste with butter.

To serve

Cook the rest of the langoustines in a pan with butter on a low heat.

Assemble dish.

BLACK OLIVE DELICE WITH OLIVE OIL MOUSSE AND BUTTERMILK ICE CREAM

SERVES 4

Ingredients

The Delice

500g 70% dark chocolate
3 eggs
200ml buttermilk
350ml double cream
75g black olives

Buttermilk Ice Cream

6 egg yolks
130g sugar
200ml milk
300ml buttermilk
200ml cream

Olive Oil Chocolate Mousse

150g 70% dark chocolate
250g double cream
100ml good quality olive oil

Garnish

honeycomb tuile
bee pollen
popping candy coated in chocolate
black olive purée

Method

For the delice

Blend the black olives in a food processor and add to the chocolate. Now melt the chocolate and black olives in a bain-marie, remove from the heat. Whisk the eggs in a large bowl. Next place the buttermilk and cream in a pan and bring to the boil, then add to the eggs and whisk to combine and pass through a sieve onto the chocolate olive mixture and mix well. Put into the moulds, place in a hot oven and turn off immediately. Leave the delices in the oven for 15 minutes or until set.

For the olive oil mousse

Melt the chocolate in a bain-marie and whip the cream. When the chocolate is melted mix in the olive oil, then fold the chocolate olive oil mix into the cream.

For the ice cream

Beat the egg yolks and sugar in a mixing bowl. Put all the liquid in a pan and bring to the boil and then add the hot liquid to the egg and sugar mixture. Now return to a clean pan, heat over a low heat until the mixture coats the back of a spoon, then sieve the mixture and churn in ice cream machine.

244
MALMAISON
ABERDEEN

49-53 Queens Road, Aberdeen AB15 4YP

01224 327 370
www.malmaisonaberdeen.com

Our two AA rosette 100 seat brasserie has many popular features including the Josper charcoal grill, which we fire up every morning to cook our steaks to perfection.

The Malmaison brasserie is the heart and soul of the hotel. The minute you walk over the glass floor the chic and sumptuous surroundings hit you like a breath of fresh air! The little touches of contemporary Scottish and local photography ensures that the local residents feel at home while the not so local can enjoy the experience and immerse themselves in tasteful Scottish surroundings.

A special feature in the brasserie, the Josper charcoal grill, has proven very popular with lone diners who flock for a seat and a bit of banter with the chefs. Three unique private dining rooms are popular for client functions and private parties. Nicely intimate, the 10, 12 and 30 capacity rooms offer parties the opportunity to dine in private and opulent or quirky (depending on your choice of room) surroundings while still enjoying the ambience of a busy brasserie with top class food and service.

The Brasserie serves local produce from our homegrown and local menu and focuses on seasonal produce from the North-East. Traceability is key to the ethos of our brasserie and locally sourced produce from butcher Donald Russell ensures that quality and consistency is maintained throughout. All of our team members are trained in knowing exactly what produce we sell, where it is sourced and how it is best served. Head chef Mark Taylor has been with Malmaison since January 2009 when he joined as Sous Chef. Previously

Head Chef at Howies in the centre of Aberdeen, Mark has also worked at the Waterside Inn in Peterhead and Norwood Hall Hotel in Aberdeen.

Mark and his team of chefs and waiters have worked hard to develop a truly unique dining experience in Aberdeen which keeps the restaurant busy seven nights a week. A great achievement in a relatively small amount of time!

Mark and his team of chefs and waiters have worked hard to develop a truly unique dining experience in Aberdeen which keeps the restaurant busy seven nights a week

ARBROATH SMOKIE MOUSSE, KALE AND BEETROOT SALAD

SERVES 4

Ingredients

Mousse

2 pair Arbroath Smokies
1 half lemon
30g flat leaf parsley
60ml of double cream
3 egg whites
black pepper to taste

Kale and Beetroot Salad

300g kale
2tbsp crème fraiche
1 beetroot

Method

For the mousse

Peel skin off smokie and de-bone.

Place in blender and lightly blend then place in a chilled bowl.

Pick parsley from stalks and rinse then chiffonade and add to bowl with smokies.

Now whip the double cream to firm peaks, fold your cream through smokie and flat leaf parsley, add pepper to taste.

Whisk egg whites to soft peaks and gently fold through the smokie mousse.

Place mousse into moulds and refrigerate.

For the kale and beetroot salad

Place beetroot in a pan of lightly salted water to boil then pull to one side and allow to simmer for one hour. Lightly poach the beetroot until soft, take off the heat and chill in iced water. Once chilled, peel skin off and pat dry.

Now square off your beetroot and cut to brunoise. In a separate pan of boiling water, blanch the picked kale and then straight into ice chilled water, once chilled pat dry.

To serve

Add crème fraiche to finish.

VENISON SCOTCH PIE, VENISON LOIN, QUINCE PURÉE AND CHANTERELLES

SERVES 4

Ingredients

Venison Scotch Pie Pastry

60g lard
180g self-raising flour
75ml water
1 egg beaten
pinch of salt

Venison filling

180g minced venison
75g panko bread crumbs
sprig of thyme
seasoning

Venison loin

venison loin cut into 225g portions
rape seed oil
seasoning

Quince Purée

3 fresh quince
knob of butter
100mls of apple juice
60g of sugar
sprig of thyme

Chanterelles

150g of chanterelles
knob of butter
half clove of garlic

Method

For the pastry

Place the lard and water in a pan and heat until the lard has melted.

Sieve the flour and salt into a chilled bowl then add your lard and water and mix with a spoon until cool enough to handle. Knead until smooth. Leave to one side and allow to firm. Once firm, roll out pastry to fit your moulds and tops.

Once you have made the venison filling, place into the moulds. Brush tops of the pie with beaten egg, then place tops onto pie and prick the tops. Bake for 25 minutes or till pastry is golden.

For the venison filling

Combine all raw ingredients and mix.

For the loin

Place a splash of rape seed oil in a hot pan. Season venison then sear the loin until nicely coloured. Place in oven and cook for 6 minutes at 180°C then allow to rest.

For the purée

Peel and de-seed quince. Place in pan with butter, apple juice, sugar and thyme. Bring to boil and allow to simmer slowly until the fruit is cooked and most of the liquid has evaporated. Place into a blender and blend until smooth.

For the chanterelles

Heat pan and add butter, garlic and chanterelles.

Cook until soft.

To serve

See main picture.

CRANACHAN TRIFLE

SERVES 4

Ingredients

Sponge

4 medium eggs
20g melted butter
100g pin head oatmeal
100g plain flour
125g of caster sugar
125ml Royal Lochnagar whisky
1 jar local raspberry jam

Custard

150ml milk
150ml double cream
20g caster sugar
1 vanilla pod halved and cleaned
3 egg yolks
1 whole egg

Cream Topping

100g fresh raspberries
300mls whipping cream
20g caster sugar
15g of toasted pinhead oatmeal
chocolate shavings

Method

For the sponge

Pre-heat oven to 180°C. Line a baking tin with parchment paper. Mix all dry ingredients together. Whisk eggs and add melted butter. Add all dry ingredients into egg mix and beat until there are no lumps. Place in the baking tin and cook for 25-30 minutes. Once cooked remove from tin and allow to cool. Slice and spread with raspberry jam.

Splash sponge with Royal Lochnagar whisky. Place into glass.

For the custard

Place milk, cream, caster sugar and a vanilla pod in a pan and warm until sugar has dissolved. Whisk eggs and slowly add to the above step. Pass through a sieve into a clean pan and put back on heat and stir until the custard thickens. Pour custard into clean dish and allow to cool.

For the cream topping

Whisk the whipping cream with caster sugar to soft peaks.

Fold into raspberries and oatmeal.

To serve

Top off with chocolate shavings as pictured.

254 MONACHYLE MHOR HOTEL

Balquhidder, Lochearnhead, Perthshire FK19 8PQ

01877 384 622
www.mhor.net

A regular pilgrimage site for Scottish foodies, the small family-run hotel sits in a remote scenic spot overlooking loch Voil in the Trossachs. As the family also runs the surrounding farmland, the chef-owner Tom Lewis has plenty of fresh local produce to work with. Don't expect things to be rustic though; the food and décor are both rather chic.

The award winning chef has lived in the glen for 25 years and is the talent behind the Monachyle Mhor story. He is passionate and chaotic in equal measure. Tom's commitment to using local ingredients and seasonality is prevalent in all his businesses. The surrounding farm supplies as much beef, lamb, pork and venison as the farm can offer and what's not used at the hotel is supplied to the bakery and fish shop. A keen forager, Tom regularly gathers wild garlic, wild sorrel, numerous mushrooms & assorted wild soft fruits from the surrounding fields and woods.

Brother & sister, Dick and Melanie Lewis, help run the Mhor businesses in nearby Callander – a fishmonger's with restaurant and fish and chip shop, and a bakery, tearoom and shop - while Tom's wife Lisa is making her mark locally serving delicious snacks, coffee and home-baking in the quirky Library Tearoom.

As well as gleaning produce from the hotel's organic plot to produce the menu, the wine list is a personal selection of fascinating bottles arranged by grape variety, plus a cluster of little-known 'oddballs'.

Tom, Melanie and Dick's aim is to provide the finest Scottish food and hospitality in the most beautiful surroundings.

When I plan a menu, the first thing
I look at is what's in season –
because whatever's in season is at
the peak of readiness and flavour
so you know it's going to
be good – Tom Lewis

HAND-DIVED ORKNEY SCALLOPS, TAMWORTH PORK BELLY, FENNEL AND APPLE SALAD AND A CIDER AND WILD THYME JUS

SERVES 4

Ingredients

Belly Pork

1kg Tamworth pork belly
1 head garlic, cloves peeled and crushed
1 small bunch fresh thyme
1 small bunch fresh rosemary
2 litres dry cider
pinch cayenne pepper

Garden Carrot Purée

250g fresh garden carrots, scraped and diced
1 star anise
75ml double cream
knob butter

Salad

1 head of fennel , thinly shaved
1 shallot, thinly sliced
1 tart eating apple, cut into fine batons
a few tablespoons light vinaigrette

Scallops

8 hand-dived Orkney scallops, shelled and trimmed
butter

Cider and Wild Thyme Jus

250ml rich chicken stock
75ml dry cider
a sprig or two wild thyme
lemon juice, to taste
wild salad leaves, to serve
salt and freshly ground black pepper

Method

To poach the pork belly

Preheat the oven to 140°C/275°F/gas Mark 1. Remove and discard the skin from the pork, put into a casserole with the aromatics and cider to cover. Bring to a simmer then cover and cook in the oven for 2-3 hours until tender. Remove the pork and place on a tray between two sheets of parchment paper. Place another tray on top and weigh down to press. Chill in the fridge for two hours, then remove and allow to come to room temperature.

For the carrot purée

Boil the carrots with the star anise until tender, drain and purée with the cream and butter. Season well. Keep warm.

To finish the pork belly

Cut four nice slices from the pork belly and sear in a hot pan for 2-3 minutes on both sides, or until golden-brown all over and warmed through. Set aside, keep warm.

To cook the scallops

Add a knob of butter to the pan, and sear the scallops on both sides for 2-3 minutes, or until golden-brown. Set aside and keep warm.

To make the cider and wild thyme jus

Deglaze the pan with the stock and cider, add the thyme and reduce by two thirds, taste and season with lemon juice, salt and pepper.

To serve

Put a spoonful of carrot purée onto each plate, then a piece of pork belly and some dressed fennel salad, top with the scallops and finish with a drizzle of jus and some wild salad leaves.

LOIN OF MONACHYLE VENISON, MIXED WILD MUSHROOMS, GARDEN VEGETABLES AND SHERRY VINAIGRETTE

SERVES 4

Ingredients

four 100-150g portions venison loin
4-6 baby carrots, scraped and halved
4-6 young turnips, cleaned and halved
large handful young kale leaves, washed
and trimmed
handful young ruby chard leaves, washed
and trimmed
200g mixed fresh chanterelles, birch and bay
boletus, cleaned and sliced
250ml rich game stock
75ml port

Sherry Vinaigrette

1 tablespoon sherry vinegar
1 teaspoon Dijon mustard
3-4 tablespoons light olive oil
salt and freshly ground black pepper

Method

Preheat the oven to 230°C/450°F/Gas Mark 8.

For the garden vegetables

Blanche the carrots and turnips in boiling salted water until tender but still crunchy then refresh in cold water.

Lightly steam and refresh the kale and chard.

For the venison

Season the venison well. Heat a frying pan, add a knob of butter and pan-fry the venison quickly until coloured on all sides, then pop into the oven for 4 - 7 minutes, depending on size. Remove and transfer to a warm plate to rest for 5 minutes. Deglaze the frying pan with the stock and port and reduce by two thirds.

Whisk the vinaigrette ingredients together then add to the reduced stock and reduce again until syrupy and the correct flavour balance, checking the seasoning. Keep warm.

To finish the vegetables

Heat a frying pan and add a good knob of butter then add the mushrooms and pan fry for 2-3 minutes. Add the cooked carrots, turnips and greens and heat through for a minute.

To serve

Place a few vegetables on the centre of 4 warm plates. Slice the venison nice and thinly, arrange on top and spoon over the remaining mushrooms and vegetables. Spoon the reduced jus over and around the plates and serve immediately.

CRÈME BRÛLÉE WITH GOLDEN GLENGOYNE-SOAKED SULTANAS, ORANGE AND HAZELNUT SHORTBREAD

SERVES 4

Ingredients

Sultanas

4 tablespoons golden sultanas
Glengoyne 21 year old malt whisky

Crème Brûlée

450ml double cream
50ml milk
1 vanilla pod, split, seeds scraped out
5 free-range egg yolks
75g caster sugar, plus 40g extra for brûlée glaze

Shortbread

600g plain flour
200g caster sugar, plus extra to dredge
150g hazelnuts, toasted and coarsely ground
finely grated zest of 2 oranges
450g unsalted butter, chilled and cubed

Method

For the Glengoyne-soaked sultanas

Soak the sultanas in boiling water for 20 minutes. Strain, cover with whisky, steep overnight.

For the crème brûlée

Preheat the oven to 150°C/300°F/Gas 2. Heat the cream and milk until simmering. Add vanilla seeds and pod, stir and keep hot.

Whisk the egg yolks and sugar together until pale and creamy then strain onto the hot cream, stir well.

Drain the sultanas and spoon into four ovenproof cups. Set in a deep roasting tin.

Ladle the brûlée mix over the sultanas. Pour enough boiling water around to reach halfway up the cups. Cook for about 30-35 minutes, until set but still soft in the centre. Remove from water, cool then chill.

For the shortbread

Put all the ingredients in a food processor and process until it just comes together. Tip onto a work surface and bring together into a flat round. Wrap in clingfilm and chill for an hour.

Preheat the oven to 150°C/300°F/Gas 2. Roll out the dough about 1cm thick, cut into 24 rounds, transfer to a baking sheet and chill for 30 minutes. Bake for 25-30 minutes until pale but not coloured. Cool on the tray for 10 minutes then transfer to a wire rack and dredge with caster sugar.

To finish the brûlées

Sprinkle half the remaining caster sugar evenly over the surface of the brûlées. Caramelise with a blowtorch. Sprinkle over the rest of the sugar and caramelise again. Serve immediately with the shortbread or keep chilled for up to 2-3 hours.

264
THE PEAT INN

Peat Inn, by St Andrews, Fife KY15 5LH

www.the peatinn.co.uk
01334 840 206

The Peat Inn is owned by chef and food columnist Geoffrey Smeddle and his wife Katherine. With Geoffrey at the heart of the kitchen and Katherine's warmth filling the restaurant, they continue to build on the very fine reputation of one of Scotland's most cherished destinations.

An inn has existed on this spot just seven miles outside St Andrews since the 1700s. It has gone through many refinements down the years but today, personally run by Katherine and Geoffrey, it is graded as a five star restaurant with rooms. The Michelin starred restaurant is not the only attraction: eight individually-designed, luxury suites offer the chance of a rather special night away.

The restaurant is situated in the oldest part of the building complete with an open log fire to welcome you in winter. The elegant interior and intimate atmosphere create a dining experience which is rooted in classical values but with some unmistakably modern touches along the way.

Since 2004 Geoffrey has also been the weekly recipe columnist for The Sunday Herald Newspaper, enthusing readers with his passion for seasonal ingredients and uncomplicated cooking.

Today, The Peat Inn continues to offer guests a delightful experience, based on values of warm personal service, fine cooking, an award winning wine list and relaxed ambiance. These, after all, will always be the hallmarks of The Peat Inn.

With Geoffrey at the heart of the kitchen and Katherine's warmth filling the restaurant, they continue to build on the very fine reputation of one of Scotland's most cherished destinations

ROAST QUAIL WITH CEPE CANNELLONI

SERVES 4

Ingredients

4 quails ready for roasting
1 chicken breast, skinless and boneless
and trimmed
2 whole eggs and 2 yolks
200ml double cream
4 small to medium sized cepes or mushrooms
of your choice
1 banana shallot, finely diced
4 sheets of pasta measuring about 8cm by
10cm, blanched for 10 seconds
a rounded dessert spoon of mixed chopped
parsley, chervil chives and tarragon or your
choice of chopped soft herbs
olive oil for cooking
40g unsalted butter
salt and fresh ground black pepper

Method

For the mousse

Process the chicken meat in a blender with a pinch of salt and
fresh ground black pepper until smooth, scraping down the sides
of the blender as required. Add the eggs and blitz thoroughly
again then finally blitz in the cream. Fold in the herbs. Finely
chop the stem of the mushrooms (keep the caps for later) and
fry in butter until soft with the shallot then allow to cool before
folding this into the mousse. Transfer into a piping bag.

To make the cannelloni

Spread a sheet of cling film out on a chopping board. Drizzle a
few drops of olive oil in the centre and lay one of the pasta
sheets, with the long side going away from you, on the olive oil
in the centre of the cling film. Pipe a 2cm thick tube of the
mousse across the base on the pasta sheet then roll up in the
cling film to form a sausage shape. Tie the cling film at each end
of the 'sausage' to secure it then make three more.

Pre heat the oven to 190°C.

To cook the quails

Seal all over in a hot oil and butter until browned then place in
the oven to cook for six minutes. Leave to rest for five minutes,
remove the breast and the legs. Meanwhile fry the reserved caps
of the mushrooms in hot olive oil and butter until browned.

To serve

Simmer the cannelloni in water for 8 to10 minutes, cut the cling
film away with scissors then place in the centre of the plate.
Scatter the mushrooms over then arrange the quail meat against
the cannelloni then spoon over the cooking juices from the
quails pan, serve at once.

FILLETS OF LEMON SOLE WITH HERB CRUSHED POTATOES, GIROLLES, LOBSTER AND CHERVIL VELOUTÉ

SERVES 4

Ingredients

8 fillets of lemon sole
12 large waxy new potatoes
10g chopped parsley and tarragon, stalks
reserved for the sauce
80g unsalted butter
300g cooked peas (you can use frozen!)
200ml double cream
2 large shallots, diced
10 button mushrooms sliced
500ml fish stock
150ml white wine
200ml double cream
diced meat of half a cooked lobster, optional

Method

First make the sauce

Gently fry the shallots, mushrooms and herb stalks in 20g butter and when soft add the wine. Boil until almost evaporated then add the fish stock and boil for 5 minutes, then add the cream boiling also for five minutes. Strain through a sieve into a small pan and set aside. Taste for seasoning.

Combine the peas and cream in a pan and heat then transfer to a blender and blitz until smooth, adjust seasoning and thickness as desired.

Place the potatoes in cold, salted water and bring to a simmer, cooking until tender. Drain and crush the potatoes with a fork, adding the butter and herbs. Keep warm until needed.

To serve

Heat two frying pans, one for the mushrooms and a wide non stick one for the fish. Add a light film of oil to each. Start frying the mushrooms over a brisk heat adding 20g butter after a minute. Cook for a further minute, season then tip out onto absorbent paper for now.

Meanwhile, fry the fish quickly in hot oil and after one minute add 30g butter then continue until golden brown. Squeeze on the juice of a lemon then remove the fish at once onto absorbent paper.

Warm the pea purée and place a spoonful at the top of the plate and a spoonful of the potatoes at the front. If using, warm the lobster meat in the same pan as the fish. Arrange the fish on the potatoes, scatter the mushrooms and lobster over the fish and over the pea purée. Warm the sauce and foam up with a stick blender then spoon over the fish, serve at once.

ELDERFLOWER AND BLACKCURRANT PAVLOVA

SERVES 4

Ingredients

Elderflower curd

200ml elderflower cordial
4 whole eggs
100g sugar
100g soft butter

Meringue

4 egg whites
250g sugar
pinch of salt

Blackcurrant sauce

250g black currants
150g blackcurrant puree
150ml water
sugar to taste

Method

For the elderflower curd

Combine the sugar and eggs and whisk together. Gradually add the cordial. Place over a pan of hot water and whisk until foamy then whisk in the butter until thickened to a correct curd consistency. Transfer to a tub to cool, covering the surface with cling film to prevent a skin forming.

For the blackcurrant sauce

Combine all the ingredients and heat until the fruit starts to collapse then remove to cool. Reheat just before serving.

For the meringue

Place the egg whites in a clean round bottom bowl and add the salt. Start whisking with a balloon whisk, adding the sugar very gradually as you go, continue until the eggs are firm and foamy. Place the meringue mix in a piping bag and pipe the desired shape onto parchment paper: for example you could do a total of 8 plain rectangles (two per person for a base and a middle layer) and four decorative tops, one each per person. Dry in the oven at the lowest setting until crisp on the outside. Store in an airtight container once cooled until needed.

To serve

Layer up the meringue with alternating layers of the elderflower curd towards the back of each plate and if you wish arrange some assorted berried and currants along the front of the dish. Serve the warm blackcurrant sauce on the side, spooning it over at the table.

274
THE TOLBOOTH

Old Pier, Harbour, Stonehaven, Aberdeenshire AB39 2JU

01569 762 287
www.tolbooth-restaurant.co.uk

The quaint harbour at Stonehaven has been subjected to many a photographer's shutter and artist's palette and one of the central characters in the picturesque landscape is the historic Tolbooth building majestically overlooking the harbour on the Old Pier. With decades of enthralling tales hidden within it's 17th century walls the Tolbooth is a modern day triumph emerging from behind its rugged façade.

On ascending the stone staircase to the first floor landing, you enter one of Scotland's best seafood restaurants. The Tolbooth succesfully blends the rustic charm of whitewashed stone walls with a distinct maritime colour scheme, which is atmospheric but unpretentious. Its reputation for serving the freshest quality seafood, lovingly prepared by our chefs Craig and Jon, is spreading throughout the North East.

We proudly support many of the local fishing boats which work out of the harbour, from whom we get much of our seafood, including lobster, langoustine and crab. Every day the 'Blackboard Specials' reveal the fisherman's catch from that morning, ensuring diners are served the freshest local seafood.

The Tolbooth is easily accessible from Aberdeen and with ample parking nearby, is also an idyllic place for lunch. With amazing food, cooked with integrity, a stunning location and pleasant, professional staff, Eddie Abbott and the staff at The Tolbooth look forward to welcoming you.

You can keep up to date with day-to-day life at the Tolbooth by becoming a Facebook fan.

The Tolbooth succesfully blends the rustic charm of whitewashed stone walls with a distinct maritime colour scheme, which is atmospheric but unpretentious

STONEHAVEN CRAB COCKTAIL

SERVES 4

Ingredients

450g picked white crabmeat
200g fresh (or frozen) petit pois
50g mayonnaise
50g chopped shallots
1 plum tomato (skinned, deseeded and
finely diced)
12 large leaves of basil
50ml extra virgin rapeseed oil
10ml white truffle oil (optional)
salt and pepper, to taste

Method

For the tomato and basil base

Lightly chop the basil and combine with the diced tomato and rapeseed oil, divide equally between 4 cocktail glasses and refrigerate.

For the crab mayonnaise

Mix the crabmeat with chopped shallots, mayonnaise, salt and pepper. Spoon mixture into glass, ensuring a level surface on top, refrigerate.

For the pea purée

Blanch the peas in boiling water for 2 minutes then shock in iced water. When cold blend in a food processor with the truffle oil and season well.

To serve

Using a spatula pass this mixture through a fine sieve then spoon the smooth purée into the glasses and refrigerate until ready to serve.

HAND DIVED SCALLOPS, SAMPHIRE GRASS RISOTTO, BLACK PUDDING, CHORIZO FOAM

SERVES 4

Ingredients

20 hand dived scallops (shucked, your
fishmonger can do this for you)
50ml ex.virgin rapeseed oil
200g risotto rice
600ml chicken stock
50g parmesan, grated
50g samphire grass
2 shallots (roughly chopped)
50g black pudding
100g raw chorizo (finely diced)
500ml milk
10g soya lecithin granules (ground,
available online)

Method

For the chorizo foam

Bring milk, chorizo and soya lecithin to the boil, simmer for 30 minutes then strain through a fine sieve and season well, whisk vigorously to foam.

For the risotto

In a heavy based saucepan saute the shallots with a knob of butter, when softened add rice and cook for about 5 mins then gradually add the stock 150ml at a time. After all stock is added add the samphire, parmesan and season.

For the scallops and black pudding

Toss the scallops in the rapeseed oil and season well. Add scallops to very hot frying pan and cook for about 2 minutes until nicely caramelised, turn over and cook for a further 2 minutes. When cooked remove and add black pudding, sauté until crispy

To serve

Assemble as in picture.

WHITE CHOCOLATE 'THREE WAYS'
CHOCOLATE & GINGER CRÈME BRULÉE
HOT CHOCOLATE & PEPPERMINT SHOT
CHOCOLATE & PISTACHIO PARFAIT

SERVES 4

Ingredients

8 egg yolks
3 egg whites
390g white chocolate
1 vanilla pod
265g caster sugar
45g glucose syrup
50g condensed milk
500ml double cream
100g milk
60ml water
40g candied ginger
3ml peppermint liquer

Method

For the parfait (you will need to prepare this 24hrs in advance)

Melt 300g white choc over a bain marie and set aside. In a pan heat 150g sugar, glucose syrup and water until boiling. Whisk 4 egg yolks and gradually add the boiling sugar to the yolks, whisking continuously. Place yolk mixture over bain-marie and whisk until thickened, remove and cool.

Make a meringue out of the egg whites and remaining sugar. Whip 300ml cream until soft peaks then combine the egg mixture, white chocolate, meringue, cream and pistachios by gently folding together. Once combined transfer into a suitable mould and freeze until solid.

For the brulée

Bring 200ml cream, seeds of ½ vanilla pod and 40g white chocolate slowly to the boil, stirring occasionally. Whisk 4 egg yolks and 40g sugar until smooth. Add ½ cream mix to the eggs and mix, then add mix back into pan, simmer until thickened, you must stir it constantly. Once thickened remove from heat, add chopped ginger, pour into suitable serving dishes and set in the fridge.

For the shot

In a pan place milk, condensed milk, peppermint liqueur, ½ vanilla pod seeds and 50g of white chocolate, bring to the boil slowly stirring constantly. Froth with a hand blender and pour into shot glasses.

RELISH SCOTLAND
THE TOLBOOTH

284
TORAVAIG HOUSE HOTEL

Sleat, Isle of Skye IV44 8RE

01471 820 200
www.skyehotel.co.uk

Toravaig House, on the Isle of Skye is a small, contemporary Hebridean gem offering an intimate atmosphere, attention to detail, refreshingly welcoming staff but above all, delicious, innovative cuisine.

The peaceful location with views over the ruins of Knock Castle c.1345 and out over the Sound of Sleat is the perfect place to relax and unwind whether on holiday, getting married or enjoying a romantic getaway for two.

Each of the nine individually designed en-suite bedrooms are intimate in character and rich in fabrics and contemporary furnishings. The lounge offers squashy sofas and a crackling log fire, perfect for enjoying fine malts or delicious wines before dinner where the finest contemporary cuisine that Skye's legendary larder can provide will be served. All ingredients are locally sourced from the freshly caught langoustines and lobsters, just landed by the fishing boats, to homegrown leaves and herbs. The kitchen is filled with only the freshest produce. The team, lead by Head Chef Chris Brayshay, will surprise you with innovative combinations and tastes, never known before.

This small, romantic, island hotel was created as the result of a dream by its owners, Anne Gracie and Captain Ken Gunn. Complementing the experience is an unusual additional feature – a 42' yacht 'Solus na Mara' – skippered by Ken, offering daily sailing trips exclusively to the hotel guests.

This small, romantic, island hotel serves the finest cuisine that Skye's legendary larder can provide. Complementing the experience is "Solus na Mara" a 42ft yacht skippered by your hosts

PAN SEARED SKYE SCALLOPS WITH WHITE ASPARAGUS, SUMMER TRUFFLE AND BABY LEEKS

SERVES 4

Ingredients

10 medium scallops
2 bunches of white asparagus
15 baby leeks
100ml cream
50g butter

Summer Truffle Emulsion

50g button mushrooms
50g sliced banana shallots
125g unsalted butter
350ml chicken stock
50ml beef jus
100ml double cream
150ml whole milk
15ml white truffle oil
10g summer truffle roughly chopped

Crispy Risotto

30g finely chopped shallots
20g unsalted butter
150g risotto rice
50ml dry white wine
540ml water
1 sprig rosemary
2 sprigs thyme
180g parmesan cheese
salt and pepper to taste
panko bread crumbs to finish

Method

For the crispy risotto – prepare 24 hours in advance.

Saute shallots in butter with thyme and rosemary for 2 minutes. Stir in rice well and add wine, reduce by half, add water, cook on low heat until rice is al dente. Allow to rest for 5 minutes, then stir in the parmesan. Check seasoning. Place risotto onto lined baking tray, 2-3cm thick. Cover and allow to set in refrigerator for 3 hours. Once cooled, cut into cubes and pane. Deep fry cubes at 175°C until golden brown.

For the white asparagus purée and baby leeks and asparagus spears

Trim asparagus tips. Cut asparagus into 1cm pieces, blanche in salted boiling water for 1 minute. Place in thermomix and puree, adding butter and cream. Mix for 5 minutes or until smooth. Peel first layer off asparagus and cut into desired length. Cook in salted boiling water for 1-2 minutes, remove and place in iced water.

For the summer truffle emulsion

Sauté the mushrooms and shallots in 25g butter for 3-4 minutes until golden brown. Add the wine and reduce by half, then add the chicken stock and jus, reduce by half. Add cream and milk, bring to boil and remove from stove. Place in thermomix and blend until smooth. Add the other 25g butter and truffle oil and blend again for 1 minute. Add summer truffle.

To serve

Shuck scallops and remove roes. Slice in half and lightly sear scallops. Deep fry risotto and assemble.

SADDLE OF DUNVEGAN VENISON, VIOLET POTATO, BABY CARROTS, FOIE GRAS AND BRAISED HAUNCH TERRINE, DUISDALE GIROLLES, SPRING CABBAGE AND DRIED GRAPES

SERVES 4-6

Ingredients

Venison

1 kg venison saddle (trimmed)
1kg venison haunch
250g foie gras
200g girolles
2 medium spring cabbage
24 grapes

Violet Potatoes

300g violet potatoes
75g butter
salt and pepper to taste

Foie Gras Marinate

8g fine sea salt
2g sel rose
3g sugar
20ml ruby port
15ml brandy

Method

Remove the venison from the saddle and trim. Braise haunch for 6-8 hours at 160°C. Marinate foie gras for 12 hours and cook at 100°C for 4 minutes. Remove and drain fat. Assemble the terrine with layers of haunch and foie gras.

Peel and cut the potatoes in half. Boil until tender and pass through a fine sieve. Add butter and check seasoning.

For the vegetables

Dry grapes at 50°C for 1.5 hours. Blanche the baby carrots and sauté with butter and spring cabbage. Clean and sauté girolles.

To finish and serve

Seal and cook venison and assemble as in picture.

SCOTTISH STRAWBERRY AND SZECHWAN PEPPER SOUFFLÉ, WHITE CHOCOLATE & TONKA BEAN ICE CREAM, FROZEN STRAWBERRY MARSHMALLOW

SERVES 8

Ingredients

Strawberry Soufflé

330g egg whites
100g caster sugar
200g strawberry paté (1kg strawberry purée and 57g cornflour, combine and cook flour out)
80g crème patissiere

White Chocolate and Tonka Bean Ice Cream

12 egg yolks
500ml double cream
750ml whole milk
150g white chocolate
375g caster sugar
1 tonka bean

Frozen Marshmallow

80g egg whites
190g caster sugar
50ml water
3 leaves gelatine
1 vanilla pod – seeds only
15ml strawberry concentrate

Method

For the strawberry soufflé

Line soufflé moulds with butter and caster sugar. Whisk egg whites and caster sugar until you reach soft peak meringue. Mix crème paté and strawberry paté, fold egg whites into strawberries, place in the moulds and refrigerate 30 minutes before serving.

For the ice cream

Mix egg yolks and caster sugar together, add melted white chocolate.

Boil milk and cream and tonka bean.

Pour cream mix over egg yolk and cook over double boiler until thick.

Cool over night and place in an ice cream machine and freeze.

For the frozen marshmallow

Heat sugar and water to 115°C. Soak gelatine leafs in cold water for 10 minutes. Whisk egg whites on full speed in Kenwood mixer. When sugar is at 121°C start pouring slowly over egg whites. Add gelatine, vanilla seeds and strawberry concentrate. Mix on medium speed until cool, place in desired tray or mould and freeze.

To serve

Place soufflé in oven at 180°C for 8 minutes. Assemble plate with ice cream and marshmallow. Remove soufflé and dust with icing sugar. Serve immediately.

294
THE WATER'S EDGE
AT THE TOBERMORY HOTEL

Main Street, Tobermory, Isle of Mull, Argyll PA75 6NT

0168 830 2091
www.thetobermoryhotel.com

Lying on the North West edge of Scotland, the Hebridean island of Mull is bathed by pure air and rain from the Atlantic. Formed by volcanoes and sculpted by ice, Mull offers fantastic conditions for organically reared and traditional breeds of cattle, sheep and pig, traceable to the field they grazed. Venison comes from the wild stock that roams the island.

Around Mull lie waters whose clarity take your breath. Small local craft fish lobster and prawn (langoustines to the restaurateur) which can arrive off the boat at five o'clock and be on the table by six.

Perfect ingredients need to be allowed to speak for themselves. Chef Helen Swinbank's recipes complement these to produce dishes that are simple yet exceptional. Her artist's training and flair for colour and form create a feast for the eyes as well as the palate. Helen has lived on Mull for most of her life. Largely self trained, she has an instinctive feel for its produce, and a lifetime's interest in fishing its waters gives her a special affinity with its seafood.

Over ten years owners Ian and Andi Stevens have pursued the policy of sourcing on the island. The hotel, formerly 18th century fishermen's cottages and with great views over Tobermory Bay, offers informal dining and a haven of comfort which brings guests back time and time again.

Head Chef Helen Swinbanks
& Second Chef Colin Malcolm

The hotel, formerly 18th century fishermen's cottages and with great views over Tobermory Bay, offers informal dining and a haven of comfort which brings guests back time and time again

TOBERMORY MALT WHISKY GRAVADLAX

THINLY SLICED - 5 SLICES PER PERSON

Ingredients

1 side Scottish salmon
100g dill
100g chives
2 measures Tobermory malt whisky
100g Malden sea salt
100g caster sugar

Method

Lay salmon skin side down on cling film. Chop half the chives and dill and mix with the salt, sugar and whisky. Cover the side of salmon with the mix. Wrap tightly in cling film, put on a tray, cover with another tray and put something heavy on top. Leave in fridge for two days, turning salmon twice.

Take out and wash off mix. Chop the other half of the herbs and cover salmon again.

To serve

Slice very thinly and serve with good brown bread and lemon.

ROAST LOIN OF WILD MULL VENISON WITH SLOW BRAISED MINI VENISON PIE AND CREAMED POTATOES

SERVES 8

Ingredients

800g venison loin
500g small diced venison steak
1 onion
1 clove garlic finely chopped
small bunch of rosemary and thyme
1 glass of good red wine
1 measure port
1 sheet good puff pastry
500ml game stock

Method

For the pie

Fry off the onion and garlic in a little olive oil, add the diced venison and brown. Add the port, red wine and herbs and leave for a few minutes to boil. Add the game stock and leave to simmer until reduced and meat is very tender (approx 1 hour), adding more stock if necessary.

Season to taste. Butter a muffin tray and add rounds of puff pastry. Fill with venison mix and egg wash lip of the pie. Add a pastry lid, egg wash and bake for 15 minutes until browned. Take the pies out of the tray and bake for another 5 minutes.

For the venison

Brush the loin of venison with oil and season with sea salt and cracked black pepper. Sear in a hot pan then roast in the oven for about 20 minutes. Leave to rest.

To serve

Slice loin and serve with a pie, creamed potatoes and vegetables and a good game jus.

DEVIL'S CHOCOLATE CAKE WITH GAELIC COFFEE ICE CREAM

CAKE SERVES 8-10, ICE CREAM MAKES STANDARD TUB

Ingredients

Ice Cream

Gaelic coffee ice cream (1 tub)
10 egg yolks
600mls milk
600mls double cream
150g sugar
6 tbsp good freshly ground coffee beans
2 measures Isle of Mull whisky

Devils Food Cake

(1 whole cake)
2 x 20cm loose bottomed cake tins,
buttered and lined
75g cocoa powder
170ml vegetable oil
200g self raising flour
5 eggs
1tsp bicarbonate of soda
350g soft brown light sugar

To Ice

50g unsalted butter
300g good milk chocolate
50g cocoa powder
140ml milk
4tbsp honey

Method

For the ice cream

Whisk egg yolks and 100g sugar until thick, creamy and light. Combine the cream, milk, coffee, whisky and 50g sugar in a saucepan, and bring to the boil until the sugar has dissolved. Whisk half this hot mixture into the eggs and tip back into the saucepan. On a very low heat stir constantly until the mix coats the back of a wooden spoon. Leave to completely cool. Strain through muslin and pour into an ice cream machine. Churn as per instructions and freeze until ready to serve.

For the cake

Whisk eggs, oil and sugar. Dissolve cocoa and bicarbonate of soda in 220mls boiling water. Add sifted flour to egg mixture then add the cocoa mixture. Pour into cake tins and bake in oven for approximately 40 minutes until a skewer comes out clean. Leave to cool.

For the icing

Melt chocolate and butter together. Boil up cocoa, honey and milk and whisk into the melted chocolate mixture. Ice the middle and top of the cake.

To serve

To assemble as the picture add the raspberries.

BAKERY

MHOR BREAD
8 Main Street, Callander, Perthshire FK17 8BB.
01877 339518.
www.mhor.net

BEVERAGES

CAORUNN GIN
International Beverage Holdings Limited, UK Office,
Moffat Distillery, Airdrie ML6 8PL.
0870 888 1314.
www.caorunngin.com
Caorunn. More than a gin.
Caorunn is a hand crafted, small batch Scottish Gin infused
with six traditional and five Celtic botanicals using pure
grain spirit and Scottish Highland water. Drawing on Celtic
tradition, we created a crisp, dry, naturally balanced gin.
The botanicals used are heather, bog myrtle, rowan berry,
dandelion and coul blush apple.

ISLE OF MULL WHISKY LTD
9 Erray Road, Tobermory, Isle of Mull, Argyll.
077652 44396
www.isleofmullwhisky.com

TOBERMORY MALT WHISKY
Tobermory Distillery, Ledaig, Tobermory, Isle of Mull.
01688 302645.
www.tobermorymalt.com
This famous, very small old distillery, the only one on the
island of Mull reopened in 1990 after a decade's 'silence'.
It has continued to market two products - a malt and a
blend. The former, identified as Tobermory the Malt Scotch
Whisky is presented in a bottle with an enamelled label.
It is a vatted malt containing some Tobermory whiskies of
up to 20-years old and proportions of newly-mature spirit
from elsewhere.

COOKING SCHOOLS

CLAIRE MACDONALD
Kinloch Lodge, Sleat, Isle of Skye IV43 8QY.
01471 833333.
www.claire-macdonald.com
info@claire-macdonald.com

COOK SCHOOL BY MARTIN WISHART
14 Bonnington Road, Edinburgh EH6 5JD.
0131 555 6655.
www.martin-wishart.co.uk
info@cookschool.co.uk

NICK NAIRN COOK SCHOOL
Port of Menteith, Stirling FK8 3JZ.
01877 389900.
www.nicknairncookschool.com

COOKWARE

HIGHLAND STONEWARE
Lochinver, Sutherland, IV27 4LP.
01571 844376.
www.highlandstoneware.com
Hand – made and individually painted pottery from the Highlands of Scotland.

DAIRY

CLARKS SPECIALITY FOODS, EDINBURGH – ARTISAN CHEESES
202 Bruntsfield Place, Edinburgh EH10 4DF.
0131 656 0500.
www.clarksfoods.co.uk
Clarks is a gourmet's delight focussing on farmhouse and artisan cheese from around the UK and Europe and every week a selection of fruit and vegetable comes in directly from Rungis – the famous Paris market.

GRAHAM'S THE FAMILY DAIRY
Airthrey Kerse Farm, Henderson Street, Bridge of Allan FK9 4RW
Tel: 01786 833206.
www.grahamsfamilydairy.com

FINE AND SPECIALITY FOODS

CLAIRE MACDONALD
Classic & Contemporary Preserves & Sauces
Kinloch Lodge 01471 833333.
www.claire-macdonald.com
orders@claire-macdonald.com
From her home at Kinloch Lodge on the Isle of Skye, Claire Macdonald has perfected the art of effortless home cooking. Claire recently launched a collection of her favourite jams and the results are delicious and attractive, on tabletops or in larders, the length and breadth of Britain. A great gift too. Available to purchase online or by phone.

LETTERFINALY FINE FOODS
Units 1 & 2 Annat Industrial Estate, Corpach, Fort William, Inverness-Shire
PH33 7NA.
01397-772957.
For all meats and speciality goods.

MACKINTOSH OF GLENDAVENY
Glendaveny, Peterhead, Aberdeenshire
AB42 3EA.
07876 474546.
www.mackintoshofglendaveny.co.uk
*Extra virgin, cold pressed rapeseed oil, home grown, pressed and bottled in Aberdeenshire,
100% free from chemicals and preservatives sauces, each of which has been carefully developed over many years.*

STRATHSPEY MUSHROOMS
Unit 4 A3, Strathspey Industrial Estate,
Woodlads Terrace, Grantown on Spey PH26 3NB.
01479 873344.
www.getdeli.co.uk
Wonderful Scottish mushrooms and deli products.

FISH

GOURLINE FISH MERCHANTS
West Quay, Gourdon, Montrose, Angus DD10 ONA.
01561 361454.
www.gourline.co.uk
*Fresh Haddock, Sole, Plaice & Cod caught by our own vessels and landed on our doorstep at West Quay allows us to ensure our fish are the freshest available.
In addition to our merchant service, we are pleased to be able to offer a Smoking Facility - through a Traditional Kiln process we smoke any form of seafood overnight.*

HAND DIVED HIGHLAND SHELLFISH
Andrew Reid 07899995600.
www.highlandshellfish.co.uk
Provides the best live scallops from the west coast, dived for and delivered within 24hrs.

ISLE OF MULL CRAB COMPANY
Croig, Dervaig, Isle of Mull.
01688 400364.
www.mullcrab.co.uk
A small family-run business specialising in fresh hand-picked crab meat. The secret of Isle of Mull Crab is the fresh quality of the crab which is caught daily aboard the creel boat 'Eilean Ban'. Once caught, the best of the catch is selected to be hand-picked for the local market.

LOCH DUART SALMON
Badcall Salmon House, Scourie, Lairg, Sutherland
IV27 4TH.
Tel: 01674 660161.
www.lochduart.com
The difference begins with our approach to rearing salmon and ends with a product which is consistently judged superior in taste, quality, colour and overall perception, as evidenced by the number of leading international chefs and restaurants which service Loch Duart farmed salmon by name.

MHOR FISH
75 - 77 Main Street, Callander, Perthshire FK17 8DX.
01877 330213.
www.mhor.net

STEVE COOPER AT SRC FOODS
15 Ladysmith Street, Ullapool, Ross-shire IV26 2UW.
01854 613020.
www.srcfoods.com
Independent seafood supplier and wholesaler based in Ullapool on the West Coast of the Highlands of Scotland - home to some of the finest shellfish and seafood in the world.

TOBERMORY FISH FARM
Baliscate, Tobermory Isle of Mull
01688 302120.

WILLIE-FISH
8 Stevenson Street, Oban, Argyll, Scotland
PA34 5NA.
01631 567156.
www.williefishoban.co.uk
Sells a wide range of seafood and shellfish, including scallops, razor clams, oysters, smoked salmon and trout, as well as smoked fish paté. As far as possible, all their fish is sourced locally but they are happy to track down any variety not readily available.

MEAT

BEL'S BUTCHER
25a High Street, Edzell, Angus DD9 7TE.
01356 648409.
Excellent Angus Beef and Black Pudding to meet your specific requirements.

BRAEHEAD FOODS
7 Moorfields North Industrial Park, Crosshouse,
Kilmarnock KA2 0FE.
01563 550008.
www.braeheadfoods.co.uk
Leading purveyor of speciality foods and game.

CAMPBELLS PRIME MEAT
The Heatherfield, Haining Road, Lathallen
(By Linlithgow) EH49 6LQ.
01506 858585.
www.campbellsmeat.com
Suppliers of 28 day matured beef, fish and shellfish.

D&A KENNEDY
36 High Street, Blairgowrie. 01250 870358.
12 Castle Street, Forfar. 01307 462118.
www.kennedybeef.com
Finest locally sourced livestock from Forfar market.

GREAT GLEN GAME
The Old Butchers Shop, Roy Bridge PH33 4AE.
01397 712121.
www.greatglengame.co.uk
For wild venison and preserved meats.

MACBETH'S BUTCHERS
11 Tolbooth St, Forres IV36 1PH.
01309 672254.
www.macbeths.com
Traditional Scottish butcher and game dealer.

MACPHAIL'S ISLE OF MULL VENISON
Woodside Croft, Salen, Isle of Mull.
01680 300220.

PEELHAM FARM
Foulden, Berwickshire TD15 1UG.
01890 781328.
www.peelham.co.uk
We use Peelham farm for their ethical producing values and superior quality beef, lamb and pork. Chris and Denise Walton run an amazing farm, rearing the animals from birth to butcher so that they are in complete control of the product from start to finish.

THE ABERFOYLE BUTCHER
206 Main Street, Aberfoyle FK8 3UQ.
01877 382473.
www.aberfoylebutcher.co.uk

WE HAE MEAT
66a Dalrymple Street, Girvan, Ayrshire KA26 9BT.
01465 713 366.
Family run butchers business owned by Girvan farmer Alex Paton. Alex's farming experience allows him to select animals that are reared in the best way to maximise the taste and quality of the meat.

MONTHLY MENU CLUB

CLAIRE MACDONALD,
Kinloch Lodge 01471 833333.
orders@claire-macdonald.com
www.claire-macdonald.com
Subscribe for £30 for an annual subscription to Scotland's favourite cook's menu club. Each month Claire Macdonald emails members a pack containing a seasonal dinner party menu – a choice of two starters, one main course with vegetable accompaniments and a choice of desserts. This comes complete with recipes and a shopping list. The recipes are full of Claire's renowned top tips and short cuts and there are also wine suggestions. Members are also entered into an annual draw for two complimentary nights at Kinloch for two people.

SMOKED FOODS

FEOCHAN MHOR SMOKEHOUSE
Kilmore, Oban, Argyll PA34 4XT. 01631 770670.
www.feochanmhorsmokehouse.co.uk
Delicious smoked fish, patés and shellfish from our smokehouse. Also fresh fish and shellfish from our own shop in Oban.

VEGETABLES

WILLIAMSON GROUP
5 Walker Road, Longman Industrial Estate,
Inverness, Highland IV1 1TD.
01463 236600.
www.williamsonfoodservice.co.uk
Williamson Foodservice sells a broad range of goods to their customers with dairy, bakery, chilled, dry and deli goods making up the range.

CAMPBELL BROTHERS
Sherwood Industrial Estate, Bonnyrigg, Midlothian
EH19 3LW. 0131 654 0060.
www.campbellbrothers.co.uk
'Today we are one of Scotland's leading catering supply companies, we specialise in fresh meat and game and have recently launched a new fruit & vegetable business to ensure our customers receive continued supplier development, this along with our wide range of complimentary fresh Delicatessen, gives our customers a wide choice of quality fresh food.'

308
CONTRIBUTORS

AIRDS HOTEL & RESTAURANT

Port Appin, Argyle PA38 4DF

01631 730 236

www.airds-hotel.com

THE ALBANNACH

Baddidarroch, Lochinver, Sutherland 1V27 4LP

01571 844 407

www.thealbannach.co.uk

BISTRO DU VIN

Hotel du Vin, 11 Bristo Place, Edinburgh EH1 1EZ

0131 247 4900

www.hotelduvin.com

BLACKADDIE COUNTRY HOUSE HOTEL

Blackaddie Road, Sanquhar, Dumfries DG4 6JJ

01659 50270

www.blackaddiehotel.co.uk

BLAIRS AT THE MERCURE ARDOE HOUSE HOTEL AND SPA

South Deeside Road, Blairs, Aberdeen AB12 5YP

01224 860 600

www.mercure.com

CASTLE TERRACE RESTAURANT

33-35 Castle Terrace, Edinburgh EH1 2EL

0131 229 1222

www.castleterracerestaurant.com

CUCINA

Hotel Missoni Edinburgh, 1 George IV Bridge, Edinburgh EH1 1AD

0131 220 6666

www.hotelmissoni.com / cucina@hotelmissoni.com

THE DAKHIN

First Floor, 89 Candleriggs, Merchant City, Glasgow G1 1NP

0141 553 2585

www.dakhin.com

THE DHABBA
44 Candleriggs, Glasgow, Lanarkshire G1 1LE
0141 553 1249
www.thedhabba.com

DALHOUSIE CASTLE
Bonnyrigg, Edinburgh EH19 3JB
01875 820 153
www.dalhousiecastle.co.uk

THE DINING ROOM
28 Queen Street, Edinburgh EH2 1JX
0131 220 2044
www.thediningroomedinburgh.co.uk / www.smws.co.uk

THE FORTH FLOOR RESTAURANT
AT HARVEY NICHOLS
30-34 St Andrew Square, Edinburgh EH2 2AD
0131 524 8388
www.harveynichols.com

GLENAPP CASTLE
Ballantrae, Ayrshire KA26 0NZ
01465 831212
www.glenappcastle.com

THE GRILL ROOM AT THE SQUARE
29 Royal Exchange Square, Glasgow G1 3AJ
0141 225 5615
www.thegrillroomglasgow.com

THE HORSESHOE INN
Eddleston, Peebles EH45 8QP
01721 730225
www.horseshoeinn.co.uk

KINLOCH HOUSE
Blairgowrie, Perthshire PH10 6SG
01250 884 237
www.kinlochhouse.com

KINLOCH LODGE

Sleat, Isle of Skye IV43 8QY

01471 833 333

www.kinloch-lodge.co.uk

LIME TREE AN EALDHAIN

The Old Manse, Fort William, Invernesshire
PH33 6RQ

0139 770 1806

www.limetreefortwilliam.co.uk

MALMAISON ABERDEEN

49-53 Queens Road, Aberdeen AB15 4YP

01224 327 370

www.malmaisonaberdeen.com

MARTIN WISHART AT
LOCH LOMOND

Cameron House, Dumbartonshire G83 3QZ

01389 722 504

www.martin-wishart.co.uk

MICHAEL CAINES AT ABODE GLASGOW

129 Bath Street, Glasgow G2 2SZ

0141 572 6011

www.michaelcaines.com

MONACHYLE MHOR HOTEL

Balquhidder, Lochearnhead, Perthshire

FK19 8PQ

01877 384 622

www.mhor.net

THE PEAT INN

Peat Inn, by St Andrews, Fife KY15 5LH

01334 840 206

www.thepeatinn.co.uk

THE PLUMED HORSE

50–54 Henderson Street, Leith, Edinburgh
EH6 6DE
0131 554 5556
www.plumedhorse.co.uk

ROGANO

11 Exchange Place, Glasgow G1 3AN
0141 248 4055
www.roganoglasgow.com

THE TOLBOOTH

Old Pier, Harbour, Stonehaven, Aberdeenshire
AB39 2JU
01569 762 287
www.tolbooth–restaurant.co.uk

TORAVAIG HOUSE HOTEL

Sleat, Isle of Skye IV44 8RE
01471 820 200
www.skyehotel.co.uk

THE WATER'S EDGE AT THE TOBERMORY HOTEL

Main Street, Tobermory, Isle of Mull, Argyll
PA75 6NT
0168 830 2091
www.thetobermoryhotel.com

WEDGWOOD THE RESTAURANT

The Royal Mile, 267 Canongate, Edinburgh
EH8 8BQ
01315 588 737
www.wedgwoodtherestaurant.co.uk

MORE QUALITY RECIPE BOOKS
AVAILABLE FROM THIS PUBLISHER

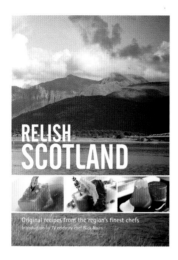

Relish Scotland – Over 300 Pages of Scotland's finest chefs recipes. With breathtaking pictures of the views and venues at these highly acclaimed Scottish restaurants. This book takes you on a journey from Edinburgh to Glasgow, across to Aberdeen and up to the Highlands and Islands. Featuring an introduction from TV celebrity chef Nick Nairn and recipes from Scotland's finest chefs including no fewer than five that are Michelin Starred. Relish Scotland promises to make very interesting reading to foodies and tourists alike.

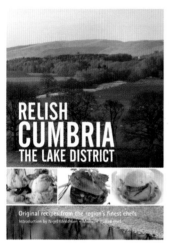

Relish Cumbria – Over 50 exclusive recipes from some of Cumbria's finest country house hotels and award winning restaurants including Nigel Mendham at The Samling, Russell Plowman at Gilpin Lodge Hotel and Andrew McGeorge at Rampsbeck Country House Hotel plus many more. Packed with innovative recipe ideas and stunning photography, Relish Cumbria makes a fantastic addition to your cookbook library.

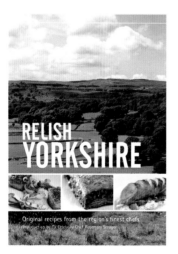

Relish Yorkshire – Featuring a foreword by Celebrity Chef Rosemary Shrager, This edition features a selection of recipes from Yorkshire's finest chefs including Michelin Starred Simon Gueller from the Box Tree, Richard Allen from The Fourth Floor at Harvey Nichols and many more. A must-have for any food lover with a connection to Yorkshire.

To find out more about these publications please visit www.relishpublications.co.uk